WHEN BLACKNESS WAS GOLDEN!

Observations from the front line!

The Memoir of Pemon Rami

When Blackness was Golden!
Observations from the Front Line
Copyright © 2022 by Pemon Rami

Cover design by Rahmaan Statik
Back cover photo Barrett Akpokabayen

ISBN- 978-1-66784-031-4

All rights reserved. No part of this book may be reproduced or transmitted in any form or by any means without written permission of the author.

P2CL • 773 599-4841
whenblacknesswasgolden@gmail.com

Acknowledgments

This book is first and foremost dedicated to my life partner and wife, Rhonada "Maséqua" Myers, and our sons Babatunde and Tacuma. The memories I share reflect their remarkable impact on my work. Tacuma suggested I write the book as both the reader and the writer, and I really appreciated his point of view because he reminded me that writing the book would reveal even to me some things "about me."

During my journey through the late 1960s and '70s, Black culture, Black Power, and self-love merged, and we evolved as a people to tremendous levels of consciousness, confidence, and self-determination. I would also be remiss if I didn't mention my mother and father for their love and for sharing their DNA that contributed to my life's accomplishments. My sister Barbara and my brothers Harold (deceased) and Barry are significant parts of my past.

I would also like to acknowledge the men who were mentors to me including Theodore Ward, Okoro Harold Johnson, Allen Collard, Charles Walton, Oscar Brown Jr., Kelan Phil Cohran, Lefty, Lonnie Hamilton, Alton Harvey, Dr. Anderson Thompson, Dr. Harold Pates, Cliff Washington, Eston Collins, Leander Jones, Jim Harvey, Alabi Ayinla, my father-in-law Willie C. Myers, and Dr. Bobby Wright. I want to thank Dr. Barbara Sizemore for her support and hiring me for my first theatre teaching job at the Wadsworth School Project. I must also acknowledge the Grande Dame of Chicago Black theatre Val Gray Ward for her unwavering support and friendship. A special thanks to Rae Jones for writing a feature story about Maséqua and me, which helped me retain elements for this story. I must make a special mention of the late Earl Calloway, the long-time entertainment editor for the Chicago Defender, for his lifelong support, encouragement, and my first newspaper coverage! I also must thank Sam Greenlee for encouraging me to write this book and for casting me in my first feature film, *The Spook Who Sat by the Door*. And I can't forget my mother-in-law, Sister Thelma Myers, and my first-born grandchildren, Jordan and Jazmine. Thanks to Robert Paige for re-introducing me to my initial editor, Margo Barnetta Crawford. Working with Margo was amazingly motivating. Rae Jones was my second editor for the book and provided invaluable assistance. Thanks to Angela Kenyatta for her excellent consultation and recommendations. Thanks to my copy editor Tia Ross, and to Lynel Johnson Washington for the final proofing. This book would not be complete without the administrative services of Anita Summers.

Finally, I want to apologize in advance for anyone I offend by not including them in telling my story, but it has been such a full life I couldn't include everything nor everybody.

Question: What does Dan Aykroyd, Angela Bassett, John Belushi, James Brown, Oscar Brown Jr., LeVar Burton, Cab Calloway, Bill Cosby, Hal Davis, Sammy Davis Jr., Ivan Dixon, Michael Douglas, Gloria Foster, Aretha Franklin, Morgan Freeman, Sam Greenlee, James Garner, Marla Gibbs, Danny Glover, Ja'Mal Green, Monty Hall, Dr. Dorothy Height, James Earl Jones, T'Keyah Crystal Keymáh, Chaka Khan, Regina King, Gladys Knight, Yappett Koto, Whitman Mayo, Ed McMahon, Lou Myers, Bolanle Austen-Peters, Sidney Poitier, Wolfgang Puck, Tony Orlando, Chance the Rapper, Harold Lee Rush, Beah Richards, Robert Townsend, Cicely Tyson, Madge Sinclair, Steven Spielberg, Sonia Sanchez, Victoria Rowell, Lynn Whitfield, Dick Anthony Williams, Steven Williams, Nancy Wilson, Stevie Wonder, and Carman Zapata have in common? **Answer:** Working with Pemon Rami

Table of Contents

Acknowledgments	3
Forward by Robert Townsend	7
Introduction	13
Chapter One: The Invisible Years	21
Chapter Two: The Rise of a Concrete Jungle	31
Chapter Three: Chicago's Racial Divide	46
Chapter Four: Wendell Phillips High School	51
Chapter Five: Discovering My Muse!	61
Chapter Six: When Blackness was Golden!	70
Chapter Seven: Theodore Ward	95
Chapter Eight: Lights up on Black Theatre	104
Chapter Nine: Oscar Brown Jr.	157
Chapter Ten: Breaking into Feature Films	161
Chapter Eleven: Directing on the Road	175
Chapter Twelve: Look Out, Los Angeles	187
Chapter Thirteen: The Hospital to the Stars	197
Chapter Fourteen: My Parents' Illness	201
Chapter Fifteen: Trinidad, Tobago and Brazil	208
Chapter Sixteen: Back in Chicago	218
Chapter Seventeen: Of Boys and Men	223
Chapter Eighteen: The DuSable Museum	226
Chapter Nineteen: Louisiana and Haiti	231
Chapter Twenty: Lagos, Nigeria	240
Afterword by Bolanle Austen-Peters	252
Awards, Boards and Commissions	255

Forward by Robert Townsend

I was seventeen years old when I had my second audition. It was at the Experimental Black Actors Guild (X-BAG), a Black Theatre company in the Parkway Community Center basement on the South Side of Chicago. It was a sixty-seat proscenium Theatre, but on that day with my nerves it felt like a six-thousand-seater. When I walked on the stage for my audition, I was shaking like a leaf, floundering with the script in my hand. A gentle voice from the back of the Theatre dryly said, "Thank you." I didn't know what to do. Feeling dejected, I began to head off the stage when something unexpected happened. I heard an inner voice whisper in my ear, "Go back out there and tell them you can do things!"

Here's a bit of my backstory. As a kid growing up on the rough West Side of Chicago, I was forced to stay in the house because my mother was afraid that I was going to be recruited by one of the gangs. I ran home from school every day and went straight into the house. Once inside, all I did was watch television. I watched so much TV that they nicknamed me "TV Guide." It was during this time that I discovered God had given me a gift to do impersonations and characters. At ten years old, I was doing thirty-plus voices from Humphrey Bogart to Alfred Hitchcock. So, when I walked back on that stage at X-BAG, I knew I had something ... but what? I said, "I ... can do things." That gentle voice then said, "Do things? Like what?"

Then I went into a zone and started doing all my characters. Suddenly, I could now hear muffled laughter and giggles from the dark in the Theatre. And then that gentle voice spoke again, this time with reassuring authority, "I'm giving you a part in the play!" I beamed with pure joy. At this moment, my life would be changed forever. That gentle voice from the back of the Theatre belonged to the man that would become my lifelong mentor, advisor, consigliere, and friend ... Mr. Pemon Rami.

As we began rehearsals for the play, *Where is the Pride? What is the Joy?*, I found myself intently studying Mr. Rami from afar in total awe. He is a force of nature. Even though I was new to the world of theatre, I knew I was witnessing someone who was truly gifted as an artist. He moved around the tiny Theatre like a five-star brigadier general, multitasking with ease, working on the play with the playwright, leading the cast in acting exercises, studying the blueprints of the set with the production designer, and finally giving his directing notes with the precision of a brain surgeon.

As a Hollywood actor, writer, director, and producer, I've done countless interviews with journalists, and they've always asked me that one burning question: "Where did you get your fearless spirit from?" I've always answered, "It started with my first mentor, Mr. Pemon Rami."

They say in business you should always model yourself after someone who's doing what you want to do. For me, my model was Pemon Rami! He's always been the perfect role model for me, so I simply followed his blueprint and emulated his behavior: the way he respects and takes time for everybody, never losing his cool and always keeping his calm under insurmountable pressures.

Also, on this journey with him was this striking, regal goddess of a woman who was always whispering in his ear and he in hers. Her name is Maséqua Myers. What was up between these two? I didn't understand it at the time, but I saw something magical going on between them. There is a saying that "Behind every great man is a great woman." But in their unique union, they have always walked side by side. In this memoir, he pulls back the curtain on their amazing relationship of love and collaboration. It's a celebration and true testament of their unending love story with forty-plus years of marriage. As my kids would say, "She is his ride or die chick." She is Bonnie to his Clyde. This especially holds true when he describes in this book about her toting a shotgun from the balcony of a school watching his back during an intense gang summit. When I looked in the dictionary for the definition of "soulmates," to my surprise, I saw their picture! I was blessed to have attended their African wedding ceremony. It's hard to believe that my journey with them has been over three decades. I'm in awe throughout this book, because of the various adventures we've been on together. You could say I'm like the Negro *"Where's Waldo?"*

Once we finished the production at X-BAG, I followed them back to the West Side of Chicago, where they created the Lamont Zeno Theatre. One of their first productions was *Black Fairy*, about a little Black girl going on a journey through time to learn her Black history. It starred Ms. Myers as Queen Mother, with me playing various parts. Then she directed me in the production of *Strong Breed*, in which I played an eighty-year-old man. During those various productions, I would catch Mr. Rami out of the corner of my eye, intently watching my general commanding the troops and sometimes sensing he was fighting his biggest battles in those executive offices above the Theatre. In this memoir, Mr. Rami reveals those battles that I felt but didn't fully grasp the magnitude of at that time.

I have experienced many firsts in life because of Mr. Rami. Among these were my first theatrical tour with the play, *Black Fairy*, that took us to Mercy College, in Detroit, Michigan, and my first movie as an extra in the classic Black film, *Mahogany*, starring Diana Ross and Billy Dee Williams, which gave me the opportunity to study Motown's founder, Berry Gordy, who directed the film. My first speaking role in a movie was in the classic coming of age film, *Cooley High*, because Mr. Rami invited the director and stars to see me in his play.

As Black men in America, we are constantly fighting for a seat at the table and for images that speak to our real authentic selves. Mr. Rami has always been that true role model. This book paints the picture of that revolutionary, unwavering, and focused commitment he has to change the plight of Black people for the better. It's easy to talk about what is not fair and unjust, but it's another thing to do something about it. As he wrote about helping to create the first citywide student movement across Chicago, then marching on the front lines with Maséqua, it touched my soul.

As I read this book, it revealed that my mentor has always been a man among men. Bob Marley's lyrics from the song "Zimbabwe" say, "Soon we'll find out who is the real revolutionary. Cause I don't want my people to be contrary." These lyrics reminds me of Mr. Rami. It takes a lot of courage to talk the talk and truly walk the walk. This book is an authentic guide for those interested in knowing what it really takes to be a catalyst for change and not just sit on the sidelines; to show up, take on whatever mountain, or overcome whatever obstacle through sheer tenacity and commitment.

Reading Mr. Rami's book flooded my mind with so many wonderful memories. One particular life-changing moment for me happened during a tour with the theatre group to perform at Grinnell College in Iowa. An actor suddenly became ill before the performance. Mr. Rami never missed a beat. In a second, he dashed backstage and changed into wardrobe—a Black tuxedo with tails—while Maséqua quickly did his makeup. It was the closing monologue of the show called, *The Negro Entertainer*, which was a poem by Langston Hughes. A minstrel man in Black face with exaggerated white lips dressed in a tuxedo comically shuffles onto the stage like that stereotypical buffoon we've come to know. He then performs a monologue about the mistreatment of Black people in America and the history of white privilege. I watched from the wings of the stage that night with my mouth agape, my heart racing as I looked into the audience of all White people looking on in disgust. Mr. Rami delivered that monologue with such vigor, rage, and quiet dignity. He knew instinctively the audience needed to hear this message, and he planted seeds back then that I think led to some White people now becoming "WOKE." Afterward, we dashed out, jumped on the bus, and headed back to Chicago. I watched as Maséqua tenderly removed his makeup on the bus as we continued down the highway. I was never prouder of my mentor than I was at that moment.

As you read this book, Mr. Rami gives you a front-row seat as he brushes shoulders with the who's who of literary, political, and civil rights activists who have changed the course of history for Black people in this country. I have learned so much through this book about my mentor and friend. I kind of always knew what made Pemon Rami tick, but now, after reading his memoir, it has been confirmed.

His unwavering and uncompromising love for Black people at an early age sent him on an odyssey to elevate his people at all costs. Mr. Rami is like that diligent farmer who faithfully and purposefully plants seeds year after year without crops growing, surrounded by a community of farmers who don't believe the seeds will grow into much and that the tide will never turn. Some years there is a little rain and other years there are light thunderstorms, then long droughts. But even with major droughts, he knows in his heart and soul that one day these seeds are going to grow into sturdy trees, that will bear the most luscious fruit. I am so proud to be one of those seeds.

On location in Chicago with Robert Townsend producing Of Boys and Men
Photo credit: Tacuma Rami

Introduction

> "You can select the road you
> take but not the people you
> meet along the way!"
>
> Pemon

In 1963, Dr. Margaret Gross Burroughs wrote her seminal work, "What Shall I Tell My Children Who Are Black?" Dr. Burroughs described the poem as a reflection of an African American mother. The poem, sadly, is still relevant today!

> "What shall I tell my children who are black
> Of what it means to be a captive in this dark skin
> What shall I tell my dear one, fruit of my womb,
> Of how beautiful they are when everywhere they turn
> They are faced with abhorrence of everything that is black.
> Villains are black with black hearts.
> A black cow gives no milk. A black hen lays no eggs.
> Bad news comes bordered in black, black is evil
> And evil is black, and devil's' food is black!"

Following the death of Malcolm X in 1964, Black artists began to answer Dr. Burroughs' question. What shall we tell our children about this world we brought them into?

I decided to title this book When Blackness was Golden! because I wanted to share the good and the bad of an era that consumed me and provided many aspects of who I became. Secondarily, I wanted this book to pay tribute to the incredible arts community that nurtured me and contributed to setting my creative path.

Rolling out of the '50s and into the '60s, Black people faced stereotypical images of ourselves which had been forced upon us for generations.

Prior to the baby boomer generation, Black people could not look White people in the eye or stand up for our human rights without the real fear of being lynched. Blacks were seldom seen in mainstream magazines, newspapers, or on television. When someone Black was on TV, it became a major event as Black families gathered around their TV sets in anticipation. In the 1950s, the top TV shows included *I Love Lucy*, *The Twilight Zone*, *Mickey Mouse Club*, and various westerns such as *Gunsmoke*, *Bonanza*, *Maverick*, and *The Cisco Kid*.

Amos 'n' Andy, the most popular radio show of the 1930s, was originally set in Chicago and later in Harlem with White actors voicing the Black characters. The television version aired from 1951 through 1953. Many Black viewers found the show was a false portrayal of the Black middle class and that it perpetuated demeaning stereotypes. In the '60s, we began to repair ourselves. Seeing self-hate turn to self-love was magical! Some Black people rejected their hair straightener and rediscovered their natural hair—the beautiful crowns of our majestic past. Some of us found European dress unsatisfactory and looked to reconnect with our African roots. Black organizations redirected themselves away from integration as the only approach toward self-need and care.

There is no doubt that many entertainers, businesses, cultural outlets, and educators of that era became committed to the restoration of the Black family. Black households with pictures of a White Jesus, fruit bowl, and Dr. Martin L. King Jr. or the Kennedys hanging on their walls found they were no longer enough. Black visual artists turned to focusing on positive imagery of us. To be greeted on the street as Brother or Sister and to see elders respected was extraordinary.

In 1962, actress Cicely Tyson, whom I had the opportunity to work with on the movie *Welcome to Success (The Marva Collins Story)*, was the first Black actress to wear cornrows on the television drama *East Side/West Side*.

When Blackness was Golden

In 1970, Angela Davis became an icon of the Black Power movement with her beautiful large afro, which motivated many women to follow her example.

In 1971, Melba Tolliver was fired from the ABC affiliate in New York for wearing an afro while covering Tricia Nixon's wedding.

It may be hard for some to imagine a time when Black people walked around with a pride not seen since before being snatched from Africa. The natural hair, the colorful African clothing, and the self-pride were captivating. I spent time at social and political gatherings enjoying poetry, firebrand motivational speakers, African drummers, and dancers. Visual artists and photographers created images of ourselves in ways we had not seen. Poets and playwrights told our stories as writers documented our past, present, and future. We started eating healthier with the help of books like the Honorable Elijah Muhammad's *How to Eat to Live* and Jethro Kloss' *Back to Eden*. Dr. Alvenia Fulton Fultonia's Health Food Center in Chicago opened in the early '70s to nourish our bodies, minds, and spirits. I often visited her health center to purchase vegetarian meals, bean soup, drinks from the juice bar, healthcare products, and to get advice from the doctor herself. Some of her celebrity clients included: Dick Gregory, Redd Foxx, Mahalia Jackson, Roberta Flack, Ruby Dee, Michael Caine, and Godfrey Cambridge.

The Black community was reclaiming its love of being Black and expressed that love in daily life from the way we dressed to how we wore our hair. It became paramount as we finally began to find our way back to our African identity.

Major artists like James Brown, the Staple Singers, Sam Cooke, Sweet Honey in the Rock, Billie Holiday, Nina Simone, Marvin Gaye, and Earth, Wind & Fire sang about the pain, beauty, and complexities of our daily Black lives.

It was also a time when Black visual artists created works to improve how we felt about ourselves and each other to provide a new perspective of the world. Projects like the Wall of Respect and the Wall of Truth were monuments to our selected heroes. Sadly, our community places far too much value on the opinions of other dominant cultural groups, and we allow them to select and determine our leaders and cultural norms.

In 1972, the original Super Fly movie was released. The movie told the story of Priest played by Ron O'Neal, a New York City drug dealer, who decides that he wants to get out of his dangerous trade. The budget for the film was under $500,000 but made $30 million at the box office. It was the highest-grossing Black film at the time and was credited with bringing back processed hair for Black men and glorifying the use of cocaine. By 1977, natural hair had started to be replaced with the Jheri Curl, which had exploded on the Black hair scene along with many other styles. Jheri Redding, a white businessman, hairdresser, chemist, and haircare products' entrepreneur, created the Jheri Curl. The Jheri Curl was billed as a curly perm for Blacks, an ultra-moist hairstyle which lasted through the 1980s. When the rapper/actor Ice Cube stopped wearing his Jheri Curl following the release of the film Boyz n the Hood in favor of his natural hair, it had a major influence on the demise of the Curl.

By 1979 braids and beaded hair crossed the color line when Bo Derek appeared with cornrows in the movie *10*, receiving credit for the hairstyle Black women had worn for thousands of years in Africa. Today, it would be deemed cultural appropriation.

My life has been an amalgamation of amazing intersections with Chicago and international creatives. I have also had encounters with some of our most outstanding intellectuals. I want to remind historians and scholars of several people who should not be overlooked when telling the Chicago

Black arts story. Amiri Baraka often referred to them as "the Flame Throwers."

Libation

A libation is defined as a way "to remember and honor those who cleared a way for us and smoothed the path down which we walk." An African proverb states, "You live as long as the last person remembers your name." So, to honor those who are now ancestors, I want to shout out the names of some great people I had the good fortune of working with and say, "Ashé."

Ashé is a West African philosophical concept through which the Yoruba of Nigeria conceive the power to make things happen and produce change. I take this time to remember and honor our ancestors and the legacies they left, for as long as the sun shines and the waters flow. The concept of libations has always been a part of our historical DNA. It has been demonstrated over the years from the family altars in our homes to the men on street corners pouring a little alcohol from their bottles in memory of the "Brothers that are no longer here!"

Ashé
We pour libation for the visual artists and photographers who created lasting images of our lives: Floyd Atkins, Ben Bey, Ransom Boykins, Mineral Brumletter, Dr. Margaret Burroughs, Bob Crawford, Murray DePillars, Jeff Donaldson, Ausbra Ford, Babatunde Graves, Ted Gray, Barbara Jones-Hogu, Harold Johnson, Omar Lama, Philemon Najieb, Seitu Rahbird Nurullah, Harold Ray Jr., Robert Sengstacke, David L. Spearman, Bill (Onikwa) Wallace, Eugene Eda Wade, Doyle Wicks, Douglas Williams.

Ashé
We pour libation for the choreographers and dancers whose movements and styles set our souls on fire: Thea Barnes, Sammy Dyer, Lucille Ellis, Tommy Gomez, Carlton Johnson, Maurice (Yao) Marshall, Jim Payne, Julian Swain, Alyo Talbert.

Ashé
We pour libation for members of the theatre, television and film community who dared to define, defend, and develop stories of our people: Larissa Akinremi, Tab Baker, Don Blackwell, Harvy Blanks, Abena Joan Brown, DuShon M. Brown, Oscar Brown Jr., Ed Bullins, Paul Butler, John Davenport, Jean Davidson, Edgar Douglas, Richard Durham, Phillip East, Charles Finister, Ted Flowers, Bill Goins, Harold Hayes, Duke Jenkins, Larry Flash Jenkins, Okoro Harold Johnson, Leander Jones, Vernon Jarrett, Herb Kent, Jay Lawson, Douglas Alan Mann, Ernie McClintock, Claudia McCormick, Kevin McIlvaine, Russ Meeks, Ron Milner, Bernard Mixon, Audrey Morgan, Marcus Nelson, Lenard Norris, Jean Pace, Ron Pitts, Frank Rice, Warner Sanders, Lonnie Smith, Jimmy Spinks, Aston Springer, Michael Allen Stein, Taya Sun, Clarence Taylor, Jim Taylor, Meshack Taylor, Latisha Toole, Norman Van Lier, George Ward, Theodore Ward, Jimmy Wigfall, Don X Williams, H. Mark Williams, Phil Williams.

Ashé
We pour libation for the musicians who provided the rhythms to move our souls toward freedom of the spirit: Muhal Richard Abrams, Koko Bronson, Oscar Brown III, Ken Chaney, Kelan Phil Cohran, Pete Cosey, Aaron Dobbs, Eugene Easton, Von Freeman, Master Henry Gibson, Light Henry Huff, Jerry (Jami) Johnson, Rahsaan Roland Kirk, Donald Myrick, Delaney Pugh, Derk Reklaw, Troy Robinson, Louis Satterfield, Paul Serrano, Ann Ward.

Ashé
We pour libation for the vocalists that pierced our ears with the sounds of liberation: Oscar Brown Jr., Geraldine de Haas, Rev. Spencer Jackson, Ella Pearl Jackson, Denice Llorens (Hicks), Paul Mabon Sr., Jean Pace, Obilo Hershel Polk, Ellen Samuels.

Ashé
We pour libation for the activists and educators that struggled to create institutions and scholarships for a new and better world for our people: Hannibal Afrik, Brother J. I. Cage, Dr. Jacob Carruthers, Ruwa Chiri, Allen Collard, Marva Collins, Fats Crawford, Henry English, Luther Ferrell, Fred Hampton, Leon Harris, Kwesi Ron Harris, Phillip Jackson, Dr. Charles L. James, Nancy Jefferson, Phyllis Jenkins, Ulysses "Duke" Jenkins, Lawrence Landry, Don Linder, Harold Lucas, Robert Lucas, Russ Meeks, James Minette, Yusufu Lonell Mosley, Jorga English Palmer, Lu Palmer, Rev. John Porter, Taki Raton, Elkin Sithole, Dr. Barbara Sizemore, Sam Stewart, Dr. Anderson Thompson, Ron Watkins, Dr. Frances Cress Welsing, Conrad Worrell, Sister Bobbie Womack, Dr. Bobby Wright.

Ashé
We pour libation for the writers and bookstore owners that captured our stories on paper and preserved the tales we needed to tell: Lerone Bennett Jr., Walter Bradford, Alice Browning, Earl Calloway, Earl Chisholm, Mike Cook, Curtis Ellis, Hoyt Fuller, Sam Greenlee, Shirley Hardy, Paul Carter Harrison, Carolyn Rodgers, Ted Ward, A. J. Williams.

And for our ancestors everywhere,
Asante Sana!
(Thank you very much)

Continued Quest for Knowledge

When Blackness was Golden

Chapter One: The Invisible Years

> "We must examine our past in order to reflect and demonstrate the ancient and contemporary cultural traditions which shed light on the dignity of our people, community, and culture!"
>
> Pemon

I was born in 1950 when Black people were invisible—barely recognized as little more than the help or former slaves. But inside of this invisible veil was the hidden knowledge that Black people carried—a whisper deep down from inside reminding us of who we are," the original people, Africans of thousands of years ago. I was a two-year-old toddler when Ralph Ellison's seminal novel, *Invisible Man*, was published. I read it in my teens. I was living the ghost life, moving transparently through time, not seen clearly and often not even seen at all.

We were Black people behaving like ghosts, as in the soul or spirit of a dead person who could appear to be living, yet dead. We were always working so that others could have healthy and good daily life experiences. We cleaned houses, fed other people's children, spent money at their stores, and had to suffer the indignity of having to enter through their back doors. We chauffeured them around so they could tend to their business or enjoy activities that demonstrated their fancy lives.

But they never really saw us. Through their eyes, we were irrelevant objects of servitude. I remember my father telling me once that he needed to take a day off from his factory job, so he went to his boss with the request. His White supervisor told him, "Niggers ain't got no business. Get back to work on the assembly line."

The 1950s, my birth decade, was the time of Brown vs. Board of Education, the murder of Emmett Till, and the beginning of the modern civil rights movement. Dr. Ralph Bunche won the Nobel Peace Prize, and Gwendolyn Brooks was awarded the Pulitzer Prize for poetry. That same year, Juanita Hall became the first Black person to win a Tony Award, Johnson Publishing Company printed its first issue of *Jet* magazine, and Malcolm X was appointed Minister of the Nation of Islam's Temple No. 7 in New York City.

I was born Anthony Dewey Ray on August 9, 1950, in the Black Belt later known as Bronzeville, at Provident Hospital on the south side of Chicago. Provident was the first African-American owned and operated hospital in America. My father, Harold Ray, was born July 19, 1914, in Muskogee County, Oklahoma. His family was part of the Creoles from Bunkie and Goudeau in Avoyelles Parish, Louisiana. My paternal grandfather, Oscar Ray Sr., and his first wife, Celanice Laborde, eventually relocated to Oklahoma. I am not aware of when or how Celanice died in 1925, but Oscar eventually married his second wife, my grandmother Savannah Paramore. Savannah was born October 25, 1890, in Jacksonville, Cherokee County, Texas.

One of my grandfather Oscar's jobs was lighting the streetlamps at dusk and extinguishing them at dawn. Before I was told that story by my father it had never occurred to me that in the "early days" someone had to physically go street-to-street lighting lamps and not just flip a switch.

When Blackness was Golden

My paternal grandmother, Savannah Paramore

I spent many summers on my grandmother's eighty-acre farm in Haskell, Oklahoma. Milking cows, riding horses, and gathering eggs from her many chickens were actually fun activities for a city boy! And seeing the stars in the night sky was a sight to behold! Being from the city I had never seen so many stars.

Once during dinner, I noticed a chicken's head chopped off and lying on the kitchen counter! This was the same chicken I had been playing with in the chicken coop earlier in the day. It was my favorite chicken and it had become our dinner that night! I was in shock and hurt at the same time and didn't eat chicken for years after that incident.

My paternal great grandmother was Azelia Goudeau, and her parents were Michel Goudeau Sr. and Marie Louise Bontempt. Azelia married my great grandfather Charles Ray. Charles and Azelia had 11 children and 72 grandchildren.

According to our family records Charles was born into slavery in Louisiana. He was named after his White owner-father Charles Ray. Following his father's death his White brother sold him. At the age of 14 he was listed in the census in the household of a Goudeau family, and he was freed by them just prior to the Civil War. Later, he married Azelia Goudeau, a free woman of color, who lived with the same Goudeau family. Our family members are directly related to the founding of the New Orleans Creole society.

Mine is an interesting family tree. We can trace my dad's side back to the original African woman Marie Thérèse ditte Coincoin (August 1742-1816), a notable free médecine (herb doctor), planter, and businesswoman in Natchitoches Parish. She was freed from slavery after a long liaison and ten children with Frenchman Claude Thomas Pierre Métoyer. She and her descendants established the community of Créoles of Color at Isle Brevelle, including what is believed to be the first church founded by free people of color in Natchez, Louisiana.

Some family members were part of the "Native Guard" a confederate unit reserved for free people of color who fought against the Union. They protected Cane River from the "plight of the Yankees" in the mid-1860s. The free people fought on the side of the Confederacy to preserve their status and way of life. Many believed if the Union prevailed, they would lose their privileges and be reclassified as Negros.

Oklahoma 4-H Club, My father Harold Ray is in the first row. My Uncle Oscar Ray is in next to top row.

Following the Civil War, some family members decided to pass for White while others would not deny their "colored" blood. My father spoke with disgust about having to go to the back door of family members who were passing. He also said if they saw one of their relatives on the street they would be ignored. He hated everything about those times and his memories of Louisiana and refused to attend any of his family reunions. Even though my father and most of his siblings were very light-complected, many of them chose dark-complected mates.

My mother, Mary (Shirley) Foster, was born December 22, 1924, in Jackson, Mississippi. Her grandfather was George Shirley, and her grandmother Mattie Cook. Shirley Street in Jackson is named after my great grandfather. Mom's father, Dewey Foster, was a Pullman porter and married my grandmother, Beatrice Shirley.

They settled in Chicago when they left Mississippi during the Great Migration, when over six million African Americans from the South relocated to the cities of the North, Midwest, and West between 1916 to 1970. During the Great Migration, African Americans in Chicago began building a community and lives for themselves while actively confronting racism as well as economic, political, and social challenges. The Pullman porter's distribution of the Chicago Defender newspapers in the South helped fuel the migration.

Mom and Dad's wedding L to R Dewey Foster (Grandfather), unknown, Mary Foster (Mom), Harold Ray (Dad), unknown, and Beatrice Shirley (Grandmother)

When Blackness was Golden

My grandmother often told me I should be a preacher when I grew up. Years later, in Los Angeles after hearing me give a speech at the Marla Gibbs Vision Theatre, the talented actor Dick Anthony Williams began referring to me as preacher when we would run across each other or spend time together. This caused me to smile and to think of my grandmother. Dick Anthony was best known for his starring performances on Broadway in *The Poison Tree, What the Wine-Sellers Buy* and *Black Picture Show*. He also appeared as Pretty Tony in *The Mack*, which starred Max Julien and Richard Pryor. Dick won the 1974 Drama Desk Award for his performance in What the Wine-Sellers Buy, for which he was also nominated for a Tony Award, and was nominated in 1975 for both a Tony and a Drama Desk Award for his performance in *Black Picture Show* which I saw during one of my many visits to New York.

Most people have heard about the Great Chicago Fire, which began on October 9, 1871, destroying the Chicago downtown business district. Legend has it that the fire started when a cow kicked over a lantern in a barn on the property of Patrick and Catherine O'Leary. Few people know that another large fire in 1874 destroyed Chicago's original Black neighborhood, in the South Loop. It began near the corner of Clark and 12th Street (Roosevelt Road) in the part of the city then known as Cheyenne, between Taylor and Twelfth and Clark Street, and Fourth Avenue (now Federal). This part of the city was also the center of a small but growing community of African Americans. The densely populated area was also home to many poor immigrants, including Germans, Irish and Polish. The segregated company of Black firemen was the first to respond to the fire.

Although they arrived within minutes of the general alarm, it was already too late. Many African Americans left homeless by the fire moved south of 22nd Street, forming the beginning of the so-called "Black Belt" later referred to as "The Low End" and "Bronzeville."

Back to my family's tenement life in Bronzeville! Tenement houses on the Southside were often rat-infested buildings that were for the most part large apartments that were divided into smaller units to increase the owner's rental income. Within these cramped apartment buildings, single rooms would be rented out to individuals or families who shared a common bathroom and kitchen. Many of these buildings should have been classified as uninhabitable.

One study illustrated that on average over 6 people occupied a single room of tenement houses. In some cases, the apartments would be shared by individuals where one would work during the day and the other worked nights so they could share the apartment. My early memories of this period are limited particularly because of my age at the time and the fact that my older brother Harold developed rheumatoid arthritis and was admitted to La Rabida Children's Hospital that catered to children with lifelong medical conditions. I remember sitting in our family car, a 1956 Chevy Bel Air, outside of the hospital and Harold waving at me out of the window. It was sad!

When Blackness was Golden

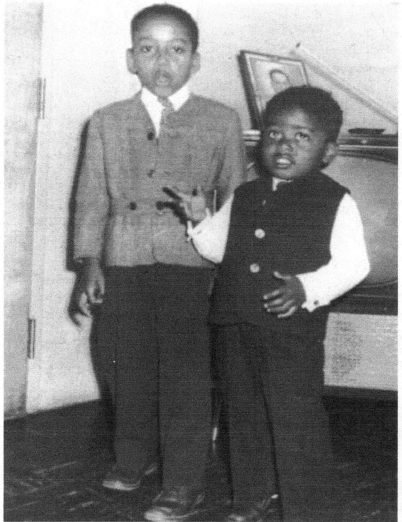

Me and my younger brother Barry performing for family!

One of the other memories I have is of my sister's bad cooking which we had to eat since she was in charge when our parents were out. Another memory is my obese kindergarten teacher eating peanut butter out of a jar with a spoon! Not sure why that stayed with me.

When my father discovered a large rat creeping into my younger brother Barry's crib, he decided it was time for us to move. One of the disappointing things about my returning to Chicago for visits was that most of the places I lived and remembered as a child had been destroyed! This was sad to me because despite the conditions placed on us because of our race, as a family, we had precious memories of those times together. Our race was also a victim of gentrification. It is an eerie feeling to drive through a neighborhood where you grew up and not see one structure standing that was special to you. But that is what happened to most of the Black communities on the Southside of Chicago!

What is clear is the city was so determined to re-claim the valuable land where poor Black folks lived, it was necessary to tear down the old buildings to get rid of all the residents and ensure other poor folks didn't move in! The new structures that have taken their places are not as well-built or sturdy and are much smaller! The next stop for our family was the newly built Stateway Gardens Housing Projects.

3651 S. Federal, the first building in Stateway Gardens to open.
Photo credit: HB-21789-B, Chicago History Museum, Hedrich-Blessing Collection

Chapter Two: The Rise of a Concrete Jungle

Stateway Gardens housing projects were bordered by Thirty-Fifth Street on the north, Thirty-Ninth Street on the south, State Street on the east, and Federal Street on the west. The site was still under construction when my father decided it would be a great place for his family to live. In the beginning, it was! It offered manicured lawns, new appliances, a park district building that was filled with every type of exercise equipment, games, sports equipment, exceptional staff, and large baseball fields and basketball courts. There were theatre and dance classes, gymnastics training, picnic areas with barbecue grills, and a small hill overlooking the park district stage.

A photo I took of the 3651 Building in Stateway Gardens being demolished in 2007

I spent most of my free time playing baseball. I was the captain of the Rockets, our Stateway Gardens little league baseball team, which my father started and managed. Stateway Gardens was located across the railroad tracks from Comiskey Park, home of the White Sox. The Rockets were a very good team, as evidenced by the numerous trophies we collected. When my brothers and I were children, my father took us to Comiskey Park a lot. It was great to see the Sox play as well as Negro League teams.

I still remember the games played by the Indianapolis Clowns (baseball version of the Harlem Globe Trotters) at Comiskey. I vividly recall the dwarf, a huge man in the dress, and the pitcher with one arm that played for the Clowns! They were funny and great ball players! The movie, Bingo Long Traveling All-Stars & Motor Kings, starring Richard Pryor, James Earl Jones, and Billy Dee Williams, was loosely based on the Clowns.

Members of the Rockets Baseball team—Sidney, me, and Jerome

Jackie Robinson and other players who followed him into the major leagues were the few Black players allowed to crossover. Meanwhile, the Black community lost an economic engine. The many businesses that benefitted from the Negro League's baseball game crowds went out of business as Robinson and other Black players' fans followed them to major league games.

Construction began in 1955 on the eight Stateway Gardens high-rise buildings with 1,644 apartment units. The total cost for the project was $22 million. Three years later, construction was complete, and approximately 3,000 people had moved in.

My father viewed Stateway Gardens as a new community, a neighborhood where our family could live among other families in quality federal housing for economically needy families. Camaraderie, community bonding, and love endured among the problems that sprouted from poverty.

On weekend nights, we would sit on the grass and listen to the Chicago Symphony orchestra and other musical performances. We enjoyed plays in the park and performances at the Regal Theatre, which was within walking distance. My brother Harold was part of a singing group that performed at the Regal talent shows. (You have not heard R&B until you hear four-part harmony in the hallway of a project building!) I got to see the Miracles, the Five Stair Steps, and Clayton "Peg Leg" Bates, to name a few. I even got to hear Dr. Martin Luther King Jr. speak when he came to Stateway! In the beginning the community was wonderful, and we had great times until the funding was diverted (stolen).

State Street was designated as the corridor of the Black Belt, a strip on the South Side where African Americans were confined. The Chicago Housing Authority was part of President Franklin Roosevelt's New Deal. Native Americans were deemed to live on reservations, and projects were built mainly to segregate African Americans as supported by the Arnold Hirsch study, "Making the Second Ghetto: Race and Housing in Chicago, 1940-1960." This study proved that the purpose of Chicago's public housing was to segregate African-American families.

The Chicago high-rise public housing buildings were referred to as the "Wall of High-Rises" that, along with the Dan Ryan Expressway, kept African Americans "walled in." The Wall started with Harold Ickes Homes on Twenty-Second Street, which housed 738 apartments across eleven nine-story buildings. Dearborn Homes began on Twenty-Fourth Street, housing 668 apartments across twelve six- and nine-story buildings. Stateway Gardens began on Thirty-Fifth Street, housing 1,644 apartments across eight (two ten-story and six seventeen-story) buildings. Robert Taylor Homes stretched from Thirty-Ninth Street to Fifty-Fourth Street, housing 4,415 apartments across twenty-eight sixteen-story buildings.

> "The decision to build massive projects like the Robert Taylor Homes in the ghetto was a concerted effort by racist politicians and whites that outright refused to live near African Americans. Well-intentioned advocates of public housing stood no chance in the face of such determination and resistance."
>
> (Chicago's Wall: Race, Segregation, and Chicago Housing - 2013)

The Behavior Sink - Rat Experiment

While working in the Chicago Housing Authority's main office in the early '70s, I found a copy of a report on John B. Calhoun's rat experiment. Calhoun was an ethologist who completed a twenty-eight-month study of a colony of Norway rats in a 10,000-square-foot outdoor pen. He concluded that this large population of rodents began to organize in smaller groups and never groups larger than twelve. If the groups grew, problems increased.

When Blackness was Golden

Calhoun built a rat utopia with an unlimited supply of food, water, and no predators. He wanted to study what would happen when conditions allowed for unlimited population expansion without adding space. Once crowding began, he observed erratic behavior in the rats, such as increased instances of fighting and random attacks. According to his study, their breeding patterns also changed drastically. While some rats shifted into hyper-sexual mode, others stopped breeding or mated with the same gender. The young were often neglected and sometimes eaten after birth or abandoned entirely.

Calhoun coined the term "behavior sink," which means there is a breakdown in behavior caused by overcrowding. Calhoun suggested these behaviors would manifest in urban dwellings for humans. He explained the chaos that sometimes erupted in cities was a product of crowding; however, he ignored the effects of racism.

We were one of the first families to move into the seventeen-story 3651 South Federal building adjacent to the Illinois Institute of Technology campus.

The elementary school I attended was named after Crispus Attucks, a Black man who in 1770 became the first casualty of the American Revolution when he was shot and killed in what became known as the Boston Massacre. Although Crispus Attucks was neither credited as a leader nor the instigator of the event, debate raged over whether he was a hero and patriot, or a rabble-rousing drunk who stumbled into the middle of the disturbance. This history intrigued me because I realized he was one of us. I was beginning to focus on my identity in the world and felt a sense of pride for what he did. My mother graduated from DuSable High School, named after Jean Baptiste Pointe DuSable, the son of an African slave and Frenchman. DuSable built a prosperous trading post and farm on the banks of the Chicago River near Wacker and Michigan Avenue where he lived with

Kitthawa, his Potawatomie wife, and two children between approximately 1779 and 1800.

DuSable is regarded as the first permanent non-Indigenous settler of what would become Chicago and is recognized as the "Founder of Chicago."

My mother Mary Foster's graduation picture from DuSable High School in 1943

While growing up in the projects, the basketball court was a center for male-hood education for many of us young men. I would hear about the sexual exploits of the older guys as they bragged about their conquests. Guys like Cool Breeze, Lonnie Hamilton, Jimmy Spinks, Raymond Price, and Crying Ugly did a lot of bragging! I never knew Crying Ugly's real name, but he never seemed to be bothered by the nickname. My mom said he was called Crying Ugly because he was so ugly his tears refused to run down his face. But all these older guys provided insight about growing up and what was required to survive.

Watching Stateway Gardens' deterioration over the years disappointing. We watched as men were forced to abandon their families and move out while gangs began to flourish. I had always felt safe in the projects before then. We had neighbors who cared. As demonstrated in Calhoun's rat experiment, some of the people living in those overcrowded conditions began feeding on each other in numerous ways, and the suicides increased. One of my close friend's brothers committed suicide by jumping off the seventeenth floor when his girlfriend left him for another man. He walked out of his apartment and jumped. We saw his body and teeth embedded in the concrete bench. He laid there for hours until the fire department arrived and pried his teeth out of the back of the bench. Children were playing close-by when he jumped and watched as the body came down—not a sight a child is supposed to see. It got to the point in the late '60s when large gang fights and shootings erupted constantly from building to building.

We didn't have access to the kinds of guns available now. People made zip guns out of bicycle spokes that would shoot a single twenty-two-caliber bullet and were more likely to blow up in your hand than shoot. Most of the fights during those days were with fists, baseball bats, chains, knives, or whatever they could get their hands on.

In the beginning, everyone felt like extended family. We knew most of our neighbors and as children we couldn't get away with anything. We also had to be in the house when the streetlights came on. A lady named Mrs. Wright lived with her large family on the first floor of our building. I'm not sure how many Wrights there were, but it was a lot. Maybe thirteen! Mrs. Wright was like an early version of the neighborhood watch. She would sit outside and keep us in line. If she saw us doing anything wrong, our parents would hear about it as soon as they got home. She would tell on everybody, but that also kept us in line. Summer nights under the buildings and on the basketball courts were lyrical, fun times. Something was always going on. But then what should you expect when there are over 3,000 people living within a four-block radius?

F. H. Hammurabi (Frederic H. Hammurabi) Robb's Black History Drive-By

Our daily basketball games were often disturbed by a gentleman named Mr. Hammurabi. He would drive through our community in his van to spread knowledge of African and African-American culture and to celebrate the Bronzeville community's African roots. His (original) mobile museum was my first real exposure to the truth of African and African-American history. Mr. Hammurabi traveled internationally, wrote a column for the *Chicago Defender* newspaper, lectured, published pamphlets, sold books, and screened films on African and African-American history, some of which he produced. His van was full of books, posters, and art. He would invite us to his lectures at the "House of Knowledge," which was housed in the coach house at the rear of the Quincy Club mansion. The horses and carriages were originally kept in a coach house building, but it also served as living quarters for the coachmen, groomers, and general servants or housekeepers.

The main house—a Chateauesque-style mansion—was designed by Solon S. Beman for the original owner, building contractor John W. Griffiths. Griffiths' company constructed Union Station, the Merchandise Mart, and the Civic Opera House Building. In 1937, the house was acquired by the Quincy Club, a social club for African-American railroad workers and their families. The coach house for the building was eventually torn down; however, in 1961, Charles and Margaret Burroughs bought the main building.

The couple used their home as the first location for the DuSable Museum of African American History.

When Blackness was Golden

Divided We Fell!

In 1962, the Stateway housing project community was informed that the Chicago Housing Authority would be splitting the Crispus Attucks elementary students into two groups based on their address. Anyone living from Thirty-Seventh to Thirty-Ninth Streets would continue to attend Attucks. All students living between Thirty-Fifth and Thirty-Seventh would be required to attend Raymond. This division had the same effect on the population of Stateway as dividing countries like North Korea and South Korea or North Vietnam and South Vietnam. It was devastating! Some students who went to Raymond joined the Del Vikings, a branch of the Gangster Disciple street gang while some who remained at Attucks joined the Blackstone Rangers. Remember the rat experiment?

Whole families became enemies. Best friends could no longer associate. If a boy or girl were dating who lived north or south of the dividing line, they had to break-up or risk their lives visiting each other. Fortunately, because my father was well-respected in the community, I was safe from both gangs because most of them played baseball with my father or my brother, who was also a coach. If I could avoid a stray bullet, I was safe. CHA also changed the occupancy rules concerning who could live in the apartment, thereby driving away many men and fathers. Social workers would come by to check who was living there. The impact was dreadful; as the men left, the gangs took over.

Nonetheless, even when the gangs began to emerge, they were not our greatest threat. That honor belonged to James "Gloves" Davis, a vicious cop who patrolled the projects and got his name from putting on leather gloves before he beat people up. Men, women—it didn't matter. He was also part of the group of police that raided the Black Panthers' apartment when Chairman Fred Hampton and Mark Clark were murdered. When people would see his car, they would clear the street.

Once on my way to school, a detective car drove up to me and asked where I was headed. When I told them I wasn't doing anything but going to school, they jumped out of their car and put their guns to my fifteen-year-old head, threw me against the car, and searched me! I was scared to death. They called me names and threatened my life. I realized they didn't see their job as "to serve and protect," as written on the side of their patrol cars, but to harass and control with fear!

The Black Belt - Bronzeville!

My childhood neighborhood was called the "low-end," "Black Belt," and later Bronzeville. It had been the center of African-American life, commerce, and culture in Chicago since the 1920s. "Low-end" was not a negative description of the people or the community, but a designation based on the street numbers. It was home to Black celebrities, socialites, and professionals. The community spawned Provident Hospital, the first African-American owned and operated hospital and nursing school in America, a Negro League Baseball stadium, the Harlem Globetrotters, the longest-standing African-American Art Center, the first African-American History Museum, and many entertainment venues and restaurants.

While growing up I walked the same streets as icons like Nat King Cole, Dinah Washington, Langston Hughes, Richard Wright, Ida B. Wells, Robert Abbott, Lorraine Hansberry, Charles Drew, Dr. Daniel Hale Williams, Dr. Carter G. Woodson, Muddy Waters, the Honorable Elijah Muhammad, Hammurabi Robb, Theodore Ward, Margaret Walker, Sam Greenlee, Oscar Brown Jr., Charles White, and Quincy Jones.

When Blackness was Golden

There were several important cultural institutions in our community, and I want to point out a few (in no particular order):

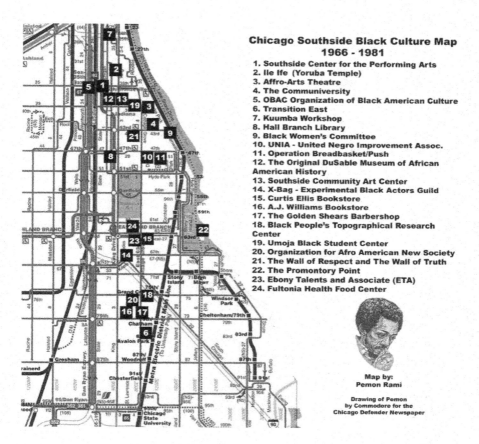

The Wabash Avenue YMCA

Located on Thirty-Eighth and Wabash, the facility opened in 1911 and was the only YMCA in the city that admitted Black residents. In 1915, it served as the meeting place for Carter G. Woodson's Association for the Study of Negro Life, one of the first groups specializing in African-American studies, which launched Negro History Week that became Black History Month in the 1970s. As a student athlete, I often worked out there, mostly running on their indoor track.

Ebony Museum of Negro History and Art

The Ebony Museum of Negro History and Art opened in 1961 on the ground floor of the Burroughs' home at 3806 South Michigan Avenue. In 1968, the museum was renamed for Jean Baptiste Point du Sable, the first non-Native-American permanent settler in Chicago.

Ilé Ifé Yoruba Temple

Located on Thirty-First between King Drive and Prairie, Ilé Ifé (which means "our home") was a Yoruba temple and culture center designed to resemble an African village which opened in 1966. Classes and ceremonies were held weekly, so it became a center for the development and interpretation of African culture. Its founder referred to it as "an alternative to the God business."

George Cleveland Hall Branch Library

The Hall Branch library, at 4841 South Michigan, was named for George Cleveland Hall, an African-American physician, Chicago Public Library board member, and a founding member of the Association for the Study of Negro Life and History. The Hall Branch of the Chicago Public Library opened January 18, 1932, under the direction of Vivian G. Harsh, the first African-American branch librarian.

South Side Community Art Center (SSCAC)

The South Side Community Art Center opened in 1940 with support from the Works Progress Administration's Federal Art Project in Illinois. It was one of the first Black art centers in the United States and has been a pivotal site for the development of Chicago's African-American artists of every medium.

South Side Center for the Performing Arts

The South Side Center for the Performing Arts was located at 108 East Thirty-Fifth Street. In 1938, the Theatre was renamed Louis Theatre after boxer Joe Louis. After closing as a movie house in 1965, it was converted into the South Side Center for the Performing Arts in 1967 by the famed playwright Theodore Ward. I became Ted's assistant at seventeen, and he allowed me to direct my first production in an actual theatre in 1969.

Fultonia's Health Food

Fultonia Health Food Center was located at 521 East Sixty-Third Street on Chicago's South Side. Dr. Alvenia Fulton, Fultonia's Health Food, provided information on nutrition, dieting, and healthy living. I had my first bean soup and carrot juice there. Celebrities like Dick Gregory, Redd Foxx, Mahalia Jackson, Roberta Flack, Ruby Dee, Michael Caine, and Godfrey Cambridge called on Dr. Fulton for advice. In the 1960s, Dick Gregory consulted with Fulton regarding his fifty-four-day fast.

The Wall of Respect and the Wall of Truth

The Wall of Respect and the Wall of Truth, at Forty-Third and Langley, were outdoor murals created in 1967 on the South Side of Chicago by a group of visual artists from the Organization of Black American Culture. William Walker was the artist who led the effort for the creation of the mural to celebrate Black achievement and African-American heroes. Completed August 24, 1967, the Walls became a hotspot for cultural activities and stood until 1971 when the building was torn down following a suspicious fire.

Photo I shot in 1969 of a car parked in front of the Wall of Truth

Affro-Arts Theatre

In the late 1960s, Phil Cohran opened the Affro-Arts Theatre on Thirty-Ninth and Drexel. It was also the home of the Artistic Heritage Ensemble. Maurice White, one of Cohran's associates who was known for his work as a musician, educator, and arranger, created Earth, Wind & Fire. When I was told a new theatre had opened, I decided to stop by. There was a man on a ladder changing the marquee name, Prince Nora. My theatre company performed there often, and I printed the tickets for the theatre's opening night.

Black People's Topographical Research Center

The Black People's Topographical Research Center was located at Seventy-Fifth and Champlain. The Center collected information, photographs, and maps concerning the location, placement, and conditions of African people in America. They provided lecture presentations concerning our conditions all over the country and around the world.

The Communiversity

The Communiversity was held at the Jacob H. Carruthers Center for Inner City Studies, formally the Abraham Lincoln Center, at 700 East Oakwood Blvd. The Communiversity was developed as a community university where classes were held each weekend. It was a think tank designed to address the critical aims of teaching and education. Activists, Black nationalists, Pan Africanists, Marxists, cultural nationalists, and community organizations gathered there to discuss and study the condition of Black people in the world.

Chapter Three: Chicago's Racial Divide

I could not help but reflect on 1959, the last time the White Sox played in the World Series against the Los Angeles Dodgers. The results were reversed. Chicago lost to the Los Angeles Dodgers, 4-2.

I was caught up in the "59 fever" because we were White Sox fans. I spent my weekends and summers as an eight-year-old playing and trading baseball cards and dreaming of becoming a professional baseball player. Luis Aparicio, Larry Doby, Ted Kluszemski, Nellie Fox, and Early Wynn were the Go-Go White Sox, and they had Chicago rocking!

The Chicago White Sox World Series race in 2005 was exciting for the city of Chicago and its residents. Every morning during the pennant race and World Series, I watched Chicagoans at various racially divided locations praise their team and individually illustrate their pride of this accomplishment. Game four on October 26 had a final score of 1-0 over the Houston Astros with the Chicago White Sox sweeping the series.

Fireworks following homeruns were a constant reminder of the power of the Sox. The fireworks echoed like gunshots through the hallways of Stateway's seventeen-story buildings.

I often heard my father talk about the 1919 "Black Sox Scandal," which was a gambling, betting conspiracy where eight of the White Sox players were accused of deliberately losing the World Series Game. At the time, I did not understand why it was called a "Black Sox Scandal." It was a crime and scandal that several White Sox players participated in who were White. I was reminded of Dr. Burrough's poem that 'black' was used to define all that was criminal or bad.

When Blackness was Golden

Like most young Black men of that time, I greatly admired Ernie Banks and Billy Williams, the Black star players for the Chicago Cubs in those days.

My father had played with the Negro Leagues as a young man and was an excellent baseball player and teacher. Because of Dad, I was always aware that the greatest players played in the Negro Leagues: men like Satchel Paige, Josh Gibson, Roy Campanella, Double Duty Radcliff, Oscar Charleston, and Cool Papa Bell, to name a few. My father would say, "Jack Robinson was not the best player in the Negro Leagues but had a college education and the Dodgers thought he could hold his temper and not hit back at the attacks they expected him to get, so they took him." Many stars of the Negro league never got to play in the majors because of racial segregation. The world was robbed of seeing their brilliance.

Mr. Ray, as everyone called my father, worked out with us every day when he got off work. People in the projects would say they could set their watches by Mr. Ray because he was never late meeting us for practice at 4:30. We went to the park often. Our uniforms were light gray with red stripes down the leg and around the sleeve. The back of our uniforms read Stateway Market because my father convinced the local market owner to purchase the uniforms. Our baseball caps were red with a large white R in the middle. Boy, I was proud to wear that uniform.

In the summer of 1959, while the White Sox were playing for the World Series, I was turning nine. One Saturday afternoon, my father took me and a group of my teammates (all eight or nine years old) to one of the games. Following an exciting White Sox win, he took us to the small park located west of Comiskey Park in the Bridgeport community where Mayor Richard J. Daley lived.

As usual, we were wearing our uniforms and carrying our baseball gloves. We played catch, ran bases, and hit balls while imagining we were the White Sox.

Much to our surprise, a crowd of White adults and teenagers gathered around the park, watching us. At first, we thought they were just there watching us play—that is, until they began to jeer, calling us niggers and demanding that we get out of their park and back to the ghetto! More people from the neighborhood began coming out of their houses to join in with bats and bricks!

My father gathered us into a tight huddle as they began throwing at us, and we ran for the safety of Stateway Gardens! My father had to leave his car behind because the crowd was between us and his Chevy. We ran for our lives as the hatred increased. We escaped without harm that day, but as a nine-year-old, I wondered what we had done to cause people to act that way.

When Black people visited Bridgeport, they knew they were taking their lives into their own hands. So, people in Stateway Gardens returned the favor. During ball games, people would stand on the corner of Thirty-Fifth Street and Federal with signs that read "Free Ball Game" parking. When Whites would turn south and park, they would be robbed or, in some cases, beat-up. Payback!

As I reflect on 1959, it amazes me to this day that Chicago remains one of the most racially segregated cities in America.

Martin Luther King on the South Side

In 1966, there was a knock on my family's door. It was a young lady named Elaine, a member of the Rev. Spencer Jackson Family of singers who lived on the third floor at 3651 South Federal. Our family lived on the second floor in apartment 201. The Jacksons were a singing family that performed all over the country. Their theatre group, the Black Heritage Theatrical Players, produced a production titled, *A New Day Dawns* at the Affro-Arts Theatre, among other venues. We were quite proud of them. The family matriarch, Ella Jackson, had an incredible singing voice and could be heard on numerous albums.

On that day, Elaine told me "King" was on the Hill, a raised area in the park at Thirty-Seventh Street and State. Not knowing any better, I thought she was talking about the king of England. Stupid me!

I ran out to see a short Black man with a booming voice speaking to a large crowd. As I made my way to the front of the crowd, I became mesmerized. It was July 1966, a month before my sixteenth birthday. Dr. King was in Chicago, demonstrating against de facto segregation in housing and employment. I knew little then. For example, I didn't realize that before the 1950s, African Americans in Chicago were colonized in slums and then we were colonized in public housing.

Dr. King talked about segregation in public housing and how they were going to have a non-violent march in Gage Park, Cicero, and Marquette Park. I thought, is he kidding? I was almost sixteen, but I was no fool! Those were areas "we" didn't go to out of fear for our lives!

The following day, Dr. King led his march against housing discrimination in all-white Marquette Park and was met with missiles of bottles, bricks, stones, and a crowd of more than 700 rabid White residents who were fighting to maintain racial segregation and discriminatory rental practices.

At least thirty marchers were injured by the bricks and bottles. Dr. King later said he felt more hatred and hostility in Chicago than he had in the south.

By the end of August, the Chicago Freedom Movement ceased its demonstrations on the promise that city government and civic groups would work together toward open housing. The Fair Housing Act of 1968 was the culmination of these marches. Even though the Act passed, Chicago remained one of the most segregated cities in America.

September 4, 1966, Robert Lucas and the Congress of Racial Equality (CORE) held a march in Cicero, Illinois. As they marched to protest the restrictions in housing laws White residents responded with insults and violence.

Chapter Four: Wendell Phillips High School

Wendell Phillips High School's motto is:
"Enter to learn and learn to serve."

Wendell Phillips High School opened its doors in 1904 in Chicago's South Side Bronzeville neighborhood, the hub of what was called The Black Belt. The majestic Wendell Phillips school building was originally built for Chicago elite families, including the McCormicks, Swifts, and the Armors. In the early 1900s, there was a racial mix in the student body, and in 1912, only four African-American students were in the graduation class.

This changed drastically in the next decade. By 1920, the school had become Chicago's first predominately African-American high school due to migration from the South to Chicago that began around 1915, causing Black Belt residents to more than double.

Phillips High School was named in honor of Wendell Phillips, a Harvard graduate lawyer from a prominent, rich family who had become a friend to Frederick Douglass when he fled from slavery. Wendell Phillips devoted his life's work to abolishing slavery and later fought for women's rights.

Wendell Phillips High School became an athletic powerhouse. In 1927, the school's winning basketball team was recruited to join the "The Savoy Big Five," which took their new name from Bronzeville's Savoy Ballroom where they played.

Later that year Abe Saperstein formed an all-Black basketball team. He recruited the Savoy Big Five as his team members. Saperstein renamed the team Harlem Globetrotters so people would know they were Black.

Players from Phillips on the Harlem Globetrotters team included:

> Al "Pint" Pullins
> Walter "Toots" Wright
> "Luscious" Lester Johnson
> Agis Bray

Phillips High School educated so many noteworthy and successful individuals that they inspired a Wendell Phillips High School Hall of Fame.

Some members include:

- Nat "King" Cole - singer, musician and recording star in Rock & Roll Hall of Fame
- Sam Cooke - soul and gospel recording star, Rock & Roll Hall of Fame
- Marla Gibbs - award-winning actress
- Dinah Washington - singer, Rock & Roll Hall of Fame
- John H. Johnson - founder, Johnson Publishing Company
- Gwendolyn Brooks - first African American to win the
  Pulitzer Prize for Literature
- Captain Walter Dyett - violinist and music instructor
- Herbie Hancock - jazz musician
- Mandelle B. Bousfield - the first African-American principal of a Chicago public school
- George Kirby – comedian
- Frances Cress Welsing - author, Isis Papers: The Keys to the Colors
- Dr. Barbara Marshall - educator (my sister)
- And me!

When Blackness was Golden

When I graduated from Crispus Attucks Elementary School, Phillips High School was overcrowded, so only sophomores, juniors, and seniors attended the actual Phillips High School building. I was required to attend the Robert Abbott Extension High School for a year before transferring to the main building. Abbott, at 3630 South Wells Street, was in the middle of the Wentworth Gardens Homes, a rival project often in conflict with Stateway Gardens' residents. On many days, I saw students beaten and robbed for their clothes and shoes. I had no problems because many of the gang members in Wentworth Gardens also played baseball with us, so I was protected.

When I discovered boys were required to take swimming and had to swim nude, I tried out for the wrestling team and was selected! I walked a mile after school every day to practice at the main building, but I felt good because I got to leave school early every day, and I worked out with upperclassmen. Michael Jones and Walter Valentine were two of the first people I met and considered friends at Wendell Phillips High. Michael was the cool one while Walter was, well, Walter.

Wrestling demonstration at Wendell Phillips with Michael Jones.

They were part of a music group called the Exotics. Walter played bongos and Michael played congas at school events and football games. I found the drums contagious. I loved drums, and they started teaching me how to play. The three of us became inseparable. When you saw one of us, you saw all of us. From the parties at the all-girls Barat College in Lake Forest to night clubs, our forged IDs got us in. We became very popular at school.

My sister Barbara had graduated from Phillips in 1963. She was my hero! She was brilliant, beautiful, and a member of the cheerleader squad and the drama club.

When Blackness was Golden

My parents took me to see Barbara perform in the play *Can't Take It with You*, a comedy written by George S. Kaufman and Moss Hart at Phillips.

Seeing my big sister on stage served as additional motivation for my career choice. Following Barbara's graduation from Chicago Teachers College, she returned to teach at Crispus Attucks, our elementary school. Barbara received her Ph.D. from Temple University in African-American Studies, and my father would proudly state his daughter was Dr. Barbara Marshall.

Even though I was doing plays in community theatres and TV work, I was not accepted in the drama club. I'm not sure why. I always felt it was because the instructor didn't like my sister.

It was 1965, and my life became consumed with classes, playing drums, the yearbook club, the wrestling team and, oh yeah, girls. I learned early how to "get my hustle on as an entrepreneur." I started selling everything from donuts and taffy apples to sports paraphernalia I printed in the print shop to sell at school sport events until I got busted and suspended for a few days. Whatever happened to encouraging entrepreneurship in youth?

At a young age, I came to value the performing arts, and I began to reflect on why the arts matters so much. But as I moved from one decade to the next, I came to better understand the impact of the arts. Chicago, like New York, is a world-recognized cultural center, and there were always many experienced, remarkable artists and performers for me to learn from, directly or indirectly.

In 1965, Oscar Brown Jr. developed a musical, titled *Lyrics of Sunshine and Shadow*, based on the poetry of Paul Lawrence Dunbar. His show was my springboard for where I was trying to go. Kelan Phil Cohran wrote the music, and Okoro

Harold Johnson directed the show. Cohran was a composer, musician, Egyptologist, and activist.

These African American renaissance men merged their artistry to create this amazing show.

The show consisted of a five-piece band made up of members of the Artistic Heritage Ensemble. The performers included Spencer Jackson and his wife, Ella Pearl Jackson, Donald Griffith, and Patricia Ann Smith, a fifteen-year-old student at Marshall High School.

My first actor headshot at 19 years old – Photo credit: Wadsworth Jarrell

When they brought *Lyrics of Sunshine and Shadows* to my high school, it changed my life. I realized that performing and creating shows was what I was destined to do as a profession.

I have often thought about what would have happened if I had seen a terrible or mediocre production that day. I probably would have followed my original dream to become a furniture refinisher like my father.

It was during this period that I became more involved with the theatrical side of entertaining and began writing skits and songs for our group to perform. It was the sixties, and many things were changing. The Black Arts Movement was emerging, and I found myself right in the middle of it all.

When my friend Michael got a job at Montgomery Wards in the Buffeteria at their downtown location, Walter and I soon followed. A sign at the restaurant listed a battle of the bands competition that Montgomery Wards was sponsoring. Prizes would include cash and a trip to perform in Paris, France. We became very excited and decided to enter; surprisingly, we did exceptionally well! We won every round we participated in. During our early performances, we wore white Tom Jones shirts with ruffled sleeves, black slacks, and white straw shoes. We were clean! The music of Tito Pointe, Mongo Santamaria, and Latin beats permeated our style. With maracas and cowbells augmenting our drum rhythms as well, our playing behind our backs and dancing with our drums was a hit with the audiences.

But it was the sixties and there was a civil rights movement and Black Power movement going on! Black Power was in the air! One day when I arrived at a rehearsal, everyone was crowded around a small record player listening to a new sound. The album, *Drums of Passion*, was magical! It was by Babatunde Olatunji, an African Grammy award-winning virtuoso drummer, percussionist, producer, social activist, educator, and recording artist from Nigeria. Through this magnificent drummer, we had found our true musical identity. The drums talked, and we heard Africa in us!

By the time we returned to the Montgomery Ward's competition, we had drastically changed our style and our look. We included more African rhythms, changed our dress to dashikis and long-flowing agbadas, and we grew out our natural hair. We were disqualified in the finals because the judges claimed they could not classify our music.

We were, however, invited to appear on the Chicago TV Channel 26 show, *Up in Heah*, which was hosted by Russ Meeks and Matilda Haywood.

This was my very first TV show appearance! The drums led me in a new direction. We began developing a reputation, performing in high schools, colleges, and at events around Chicago and neighboring states, and we became a much sought-after group. Even though I was underage, I was invited to play with several adult bands in nightclubs around the city. I was too young to sit in the club, so I would usually have to wait in a storage room or office until we started playing. Playing percussions with alto saxophonist Troy Robinson's jazz band was one of my favorite music gigs when I was sixteen and seventeen. Troy had a space on the corner of Seventy-Sixth and Cottage Grove, called the Troy Robinson Workshop. Troy Robinson eventually left Chicago for Los Angeles to pursue work in the entertainment industry and for music-arranging gigs.

Ilé Ifé, A Yoruba Temple

Every Friday night, Ilé Ifé held an African ceremony called a bemba where we played along with several other drummers. Ancestorial connections played a central role in the Bembé. Rituals were performed to seek their assistance and ask for guidance.

Baba Alabi Ayinla was the Yoruba priest who presided over the temple. Aside from learning about the Yoruba culture, rituals, and language, we also participated in the sacrifice of chickens and white rats for cleansing. The animals' blood would be mixed with rum and passed around to participants.

When I wasn't playing at Ilé Ifé, I would play with one of the bands I worked with. When we played at a club in Gary,

When Blackness was Golden

Indiana and it was time to get paid, I was told the band members had drunk up our payment! Struggling home in the snow with my drums that night helped me decide to stop drumming! I reflected later, if I had been a flute player, I may still be a musician. Instead, I had a set of heavy drums!

We were constantly involved in touring productions to provide cultural exposure and self-repair. We performed on tour with Erskine Coleman, who owned the Golden Shears Barbershop. The shop gained its name because of the 14-karat golden shears award he won cutting natural hair, which was a big deal among Black barbers in the '60s and '70s. Erskine's barbershop on Seventy-Ninth Street would demonstrate Afro haircuts and hold African fashion shows. Our group, the Exotics, provided the entertainment, and Curtis Ellis of Ellis Bookstore would have Black books for sale. We came together to present Black cultural shows, so culture would become a part of the collective vision of what our people needed to create a social movement.

I was moving closer to the views of Malcolm X. My peers and I listened to his albums intensely. *Message to the Grassroots* and *the Ballot or the Bullet* albums became a must! Malcolm X shared that James Baldwin was to speak once in Paris, France, but it was decided that he had to let Burt Lancaster (or someone) read the speech, for it was feared that Baldwin would go off-script. I learned from Malcolm that expressing my voice was paramount in all that I do. I decided I would "do a great deal."

Our self-education included reading the books of Honorable Marcus Garvey, Frantz Fanon, Richard Wright, Lerone Bennett, LeRoi Jones (Amiri Baraka), W. E. B. Dubois, Che Guevara, Chancellor Williams, and James Baldwin, to name a few. My book collection as a teenager included *The Autobiography of Malcolm X*, Lerone Bennett's *Before the Mayflower*, Eldridge Cleaver's *Soul on Ice*, Bobby Seale's *Seize the Time*, and Kwame Touré's (Stokely Carmichael) and Charles Hamilton's *Black Power: The Politics of Liberation*.

I also had a collection of Black plays by Ed Bullins, Ted Ward, Ron Milner, Langston Hughes, James Baldwin, Richard Wesly, Joseph Walker, Oscar Brown Jr., Bill Harris, William Electric Black, Douglas Turner Ward, and numerous Black theatre anthologies.

Chapter Five: Discovering My Muse!

I first met Rhonada Angelia Myers on March 29, 1968, when she walked into the auditorium at Calumet High School in the Auburn Gresham community on Eighty-First and May. It was an interesting neighborhood because during the decade from 1960 to 1970, the population had flipped to 70 percent middle-class African Americans. I took my mind off sociology of the South Side when Rhonada walked in the room while we were setting up for our performance.

Maséqua's Calumet High School senior photo

Rhonada had big legs, an infectious smile, and beautiful natural hair. It was long in the back and reminded me of a lion's mane. She had the image of a young African queen. I had been invited to Calumet High School with my drum/acting company to perform Langston Hughes' "Jesse B. Simple" skits and poetry to drum music.

Oscar Brown Jr.'s 1961 album, *Sin and Soul*, included the songs *"But I Was Cool," "Signifyin' Monkey," and "Somebody Buy Me a Drink,"* which represented what we were evolving into. He was a poet, a playwright, a director, a musician, a singer, and an activist.

Activists were thinkers voicing their views of commitment to full equality and social change—the opposite of the old-fashioned attitude, "I'm going along with the man to get along." This new perspective propelled us to higher levels of creativity and mental freedom. We worked to redefine every domain of culture to reflect our world views and our art. Language, for example, became what we wanted it to be to represent our voices.

The roots of rap and hip-hop grew from the African griot who told the stories of their community through music and language. One such poet was South African poet Keorapetse Kgositsile who put his poems to drums in the late 1960s. He briefly attended Lincoln University before moving to New York where he joined the staff of *Black Dialogue* magazine. In New York, he reunited with his friends Hugh Masekela and Jonas Gwangwa, prominent South African jazz musicians who were living in exile, and befriended a coterie of Harlem-based writers, including Amiri Baraka (then known as LeRoi Jones) and Ishmael Reed.

The Original Last Poets and Gil Scott Heron heard this South African brother and transplanted those sounds in their work. We grew like oak trees in remodeling language in our music. Our styles of singing were the predecessors to rap music.

When Blackness was Golden

The day I met Rhonada, I recall so vividly because our performance received a standing ovation from the students at Calumet, and it was one week before Dr. Martin Luther King Jr. was assassinated. Dr. King was speaking out against the Vietnam War and calling for a radical, economic, non-violent revolution to support the Poor People's Campaign. These, his next-level targets, were probably why he was killed.

Chicago and African-American communities nationwide exploded on April 4, 1968, when Dr. King was murdered! Curfews, National Guard, and Chicago's West Side lit up.

African Americans had made quantum leaps in racial pride following the death of Malcolm X. After King's assassination in Memphis, Tennessee, following the tears and anger came greater purpose. Dr. King's legacy further impacted our lives.

Rhonada was the vice president of C.A.S.O., Calumet High School's Afro-American Student Organization, and she was on the committee that had planned our visit to the school. I was so impressed with her! She was smart, outspoken, beautiful, feisty, dark-chocolate and highly respected by her peers.

As always after our group performed, I started recruiting people to join our troupe or classes. As they exited, I asked people to sign our sign-up sheet. When Rhonada walked up to the table, I asked her to put a star next to her name so that I would be sure to call her back. I thought that was a great ploy.

Chaka Khan and Maséqua, 1968

Rhonada, along with some of her planning group members, convened to Foster Park. My group played congas while Rhonada and classmates Zuri, Mokeyé, and Yvette Stevens (later to become Chaka Khan), sang and danced to the beat. Chaka's first group sang together under the auspices of *"Shades of Black,"* taken from my show I produced at Stateway Park's field house titled *Shades of Black Beauty*. Chaka was a member of the cast.

I had planned to call Rhonada the next day so we could meet at a rally that weekend. Later that evening after leaving the park, I was shot in the back. At first, I didn't know I was shot because I only felt I'd been hit by something in my back. I continued walking, but my back burned, and then I noticed the blood. As leaders of the Black student movement, we had been warned by an informant that our lives were in danger.

I was taken to Cook County Hospital. Someone called my mother and told her I was dead! It wasn't until my family arrived at the hospital that they discovered it wasn't true. I later realized I had lost my briefcase with my phone book and all the numbers I had collected that day, so I couldn't call Rhonada or anyone else.

A few months later, while still recovering, I was living in my parents' apartment in Stateway. I walked to the store to get some fresh air. I had been cooped up for weeks. Who do I see walking down State Street? Rhonada! She was on her way to volunteer at the campaign office of A. A. Raynor

When Blackness was Golden

who was running for political office against Ralph Metcalfe Sr., an ally of Mayor Daley. I believed it was destiny that we met again.

Rhonada and I started dating shortly after that fateful day—that is, if you can call attending rallies, meetings, demonstrations, political events, and protests—dates! We even participated in the development and recording of Rayner's campaign radio commercial:

> Said Daley: "Shoot to kill!"
> Said Metcalfe: "I'll load the gun!"
> Said Daley: I need an errand boy!"
> Said Metcalfe: "I sure can run!"
> Said Daley: "There's a rumbling on the ground!"
> Said Metcalfe: I'll keep those Black folks down!"
> Vote for Rayner!

The commercial played on local radio stations in Chicago.

Our activism gave us constructive time together and a chance to really get to know what we believed in and stood for.

My civil rights involvement paralleled my work in the arts. Like one of my mentors, the legendary entertainer and civil rights activist Oscar Brown, Jr., I was on my way to evolving in the areas he starred in. I was playing music, producing plays, planning, and participating in demonstrations all at the same time.

I first went to visit Rhonada at her family's apartment on the second story of a two flat in the upscale Auburn Gresham district on the South Side. I was impressed by the manicured lawns, clean alleys, and well-to-do Black folks living in a rapidly changing area. As whites fled the community, Blacks moved in.

I loved her family right away! Her mom and dad were members of the Congress for Racial Equality and immersed in the church and civil rights movement. When I met them, Maséqua's mother was a nurse at Cook County VA Hospital. Sister T. M. Myers, as she is often referred, later worked at Roosevelt University with the Upward Bound program students and came to be recognized as a mentor and mother to many.

Rhonada's eighty-three-year-old grandmother, Ma Maggie (Trotter), lived with her along with her brothers Raybon and Relman. (Her parents had a thing for starting their children's names with the same letter.) And there was George, a squirrel monkey they had as a pet! Freaked me out! Maséqua's father, Willie C. Myers, was the first African-American zookeeper at Lincoln Park Zoo, which explained the hawks, rabbits, turtles, and snakes he would bring home to care for. While my family was not involved in the civil rights movement, her family was very committed and active.

When I received my African name while involved with Ilé Ifé, I also asked for a name that I could give to my future wife. I was given "Maséqua" which means queen of a darker hue. Shortly after I met Rhonada, I knew she deserved that name. I discussed the name with her and, after she discussed it with her parents, she accepted it.

A few months later, as one of the leaders of the Umoja Black Student Center, I was invited to participate at the National Black Power Conference in Philadelphia, being held at the historic Church of the Advocate in the heart of North Philadelphia. Maséqua told me her family was going to attend, and I asked if I could ride with them. Her mother said if my father approved, it would be OK. I explained to her I was eighteen and grown and he would not mind, but she demanded they talk anyway. My father said exactly what I told her he would, and I got to ride with them.

When Blackness was Golden

One night during the conference, the student workshop ran late. Maséqua and I ended up walking back to where we were staying with her father's sister in West Philly. We took what we thought was a shortcut, which happened to pass through a cemetery between the Church of the Advocate and the house on Girard Avenue. It was like something out of a horror movie scene.

When we arrived at the house, Maséqua's father was standing on the front porch, and he was livid! He was concerned for his daughter and kept me on the porch talking about his expectations of how I should treat his daughter and how we should have come straight home. He had just met me, so I understood. We ended up having a great conversation. Mr. Myers was a wonderful spirit. He was hardworking, generous, and kind. He would come to my apartment when I had card parties and tell everyone, "Watch out because I cheat!" But we could never catch him cheating. I became so close to Maséqua's family that people meeting us thought I was her brother.

Maséqua and me at her Aunt Bertha Baskins' house in Joliet, IL

In 1969, I directed Benjamin Caldwell's play, Prayer Meeting, or The First Militant Minister at the Abraham Lincoln Center. Mr. Othello Ellis headed the center for twenty-one years and encouraged my development by letting me use the theatre whenever I needed it.

The short play is about a burglar looting a minister's home. When the weary minister returns home unexpectedly, he begins to pray. From his hiding place, the burglar tells him

With Maséqua Myers-Rami, Tiamoyo Karenga, and Dr. Maulana Karenga

to shut up and get off his knees. He then realizes that the minister believes God has answered him. The burglar proceeds to convince the minister he needs to be more militant and join the people in their struggle for liberation. Our guest speaker at the show that night was Maulana Ron Karenga, the founder of Kwanzaa. I was on my way to building the creative life I envisioned in my mind and spirit. The Kawaida principles created by Dr. Maulana Karenga became part of my thought, our daily practices, and contributed to our identities as cultural nationalists. My future productions evolved from our involvement in the cultural revolution of the 1960s and '70s, the Black Arts Movement. Our creative life together was just beginning!

Maséqua with me in a scene from the play *Ododo* by Joseph Walker

Chapter Six: When Blackness was Golden!

> "Don't allow yourself to believe your
> natural beauty requires augmentation
> to change you into a diminished
> version of another cultural group."
>
> Pemon

When Maséqua and I met, I had already begun working with Jim Harvey on opening the Umoja Black Student Center at 251 East Thirty-Ninth Street, directly across from Wendell Phillips High School. By the early '70s, Afro-American student movements were springing to life everywhere—on campuses, in high schools, and in communities. Students were affirming new demands and priorities. The birth and direction of the Umoja Black Student Center needed young leadership, and I gladly took on one of those roles.

I had contacts at many of the high schools and colleges citywide through my performing company, which made recruitment easier. Umoja opened as a cultural center and home for Black students.

The Umoja Black Student Center was governed by a central committee with twelve members, including me, who decided on the efforts and philosophy of the organization as well as which activities we would become involved with. I was the coordinator of the Black Students for Defense (one of the sub-groups) of the Afro-American Student Association.

The Umoja Black Student Center reflected this multicultural programming. It was the home for African-American teens and adults in Chicago trying to find themselves.

When Blackness was Golden

Black History, culture, manhood, womanhood, Swahili, karate, and self-defense classes were among our offerings.

In November 1967, Englewood High School became the epicenter of our efforts when Owen Lawson, a teacher who insisted on including Black history in his lesson plans, was dismissed. We met with the students, helped them develop their strategies, and even cut or styled their hair for those who wanted to wear their hair natural. Englewood students held walkouts and protests but despite their efforts, Owen was not reinstated. Lawson's struggle demonstrated the need for more Black control of our schools and, more specifically, our education.

Broadcast veteran Harold Lee Rush, one of the student leaders at Englewood during that time, became a good friend and joined my acting group.

One of my personal objectives while performing at various schools and community functions was to recruit members and to conjoin the variety of school organizations to find leaders who could help us organize people. I was able to enlist many individuals to join our efforts, which impacted the rest of the movement. I grew to understand the skills and work of activists and the powerful role they played in any community, city, or country.

The third Black Power conference was held at the historic Church of the Advocate in the heart of North Philadelphia from Wednesday, August 28 to Sunday, September 1, 1968. The conference drew over 4,000 people, far exceeding the building's capacity.

The conference theme was "Black self-determination and unity through direct action." Attendees included Max Stanford, Queen Mother Moore, Maulana Karenga, Amiri Baraka, Jesse Jackson, Whitney Young, Nathan Hare, John Conyers, and Rosa Parks, to name a few. We organized ten workshops around politics, education, culture, history, economics, reparations, Black women community organizing, religion, communication, and education.

Maséqua and I co-chaired the high school student workshop. One of the defined outcomes was a plan to return to our respective cities and schools to organize a movement to create major changes needed in the educational system.

When Blackness was Golden

In many ways, the current Black Lives Matter movement is the contemporary version of our movement in terms of youth leading the action in the streets.

While I was in Philadelphia for the conference on Thursday, August 29, five members of the emergency consultative committee held a midnight meeting at the Umoja Center to discuss the results of action taken around the Democratic Convention and the condition of the police state in Chicago. During the meeting, multiple shots were fired into the building. Members scrambled for their lives. The chairman of the Umoja Center, Jim Harvey, remarked, "The attack was an extension of the racist war on Black students seeking self-determination for all Black people."

The Chicago Student Movement

When I returned to Chicago, we learned of the shooting at the center and that one of our members had been murdered a few days later. I immediately began reaching out to other students and organizing small gatherings to share the conference outcomes and events. In the fall of 1968, student protests began at Austin and Harrison High Schools. We saw these protests as opportunities to move forward.

On Sunday, October 13, 1968, I organized a final meeting before the boycott of twenty-five representatives from more than thirteen Chicago high schools at the Umoja Black Student Center. The purpose of the meeting was to consolidate growing protests at numerous high schools and to form the Black Students for Defense subgroup of the Afro-American Student Organization to organize our collective demands and demonstrations. I was selected coordinator.

Me addressing the press at the CPS mock funeral with Maséqua and her brother Relman ST-11006287-0001, Chicago Sun-Times collection, Chicago History Museum

High schools represented included Calumet, Chicago Vocational, Dunbar, DuSable, Englewood, Harlan, Harrison, Lindblom, Marshall, Parker, Wendell Phillips, Simeon, and South Shore. During the meeting, we set plans into motion for a citywide school boycott and distributed copies of the manifesto containing twelve demands, most of which were developed during the student workshop at the National Black Power conference. We attended a meeting at the Board of Education to submit our series of demands that we called the Black Manifesto.

Black Manifesto Demands

1. Complete courses in Black history
2. Inclusion in all courses the contributions of Black persons
3. Black administration in schools in the Black communities
4. More technical and vocational training
5. More Black teachers
6. Repair of school buildings in Black communities
7. Holidays on the birthdays of such Black heroes as Marcus Garvey, Malcolm X, W. E. B. DuBois, and Dr. Martin Luther King Jr.
8. Insurance for athletes
9. Use of Black businesses to supply class photos and rings in Black schools
10. Better cafeteria food
11. Military training relevant to Black people's needs
12. More required homework to challenge Black students

When our demands were not seriously addressed, we set the boycotts in motion. The first citywide boycott took place on Monday, October 14, 1968. According to published reports, between 27,000 and 35,000 students stayed out of school. We held a rally at the Affro-Arts Theatre and then marched to Washington Park, where I addressed the large crowd along with Jim Harvey, Victor Adams, and Russ Meeks. We decided to only boycott school on Mondays because we wanted to demonstrate we were still interested in receiving an education.

Maséqua and me in the middle of the student march, 1968

Me in the Beret!

October 28, 1968, we held a mock funeral of the Board of Education at Civic Plaza. Using my theatre technical skills, I made a coffin which was carried in a processional to the Civic Center. At a designated time, Victor Adams and I ran across the Plaza and jumped on the coffin, destroying it! Some students wore black Ku Klux Klan robes as they silently carried the coffin.

The picture of us jumping on the coffin appeared in Ebony magazine and was the week's best photo in Jet magazine in a November 1968 issue. In the photo, I was caught in the air over the coffin wearing a black beret. Victor Adams is positioned with his back to the camera, and Sharron Matthews a student leader from Harrison High School is standing in the background.

Famed Chicago journalist and writer Lou Palmer was one of the reporters assigned to cover the student movement by the *Chicago Daily* newspaper because we would not allow White journalists to attend our meetings and rallies. Other media outlets followed suit and hired Warner Sanders and Vernon Jarrett, among others. My first series of meetings with the Rev. Jesse Jackson over the years was at Umoja Black Student Center. He arranged a meeting to convince me to make hiring of Black businesses our number one priority, which would garner his support for the boycott. I respectfully declined because we felt all the issues, we presented were important, and Black businesses were not at the top of our list of priorities.

On October 30, 1968, we met with the Board of Education and submitted our final demands. As anyone who has worked with large groups of people will testify, organizing is not easy! We needed large numbers of students to become involved in our struggle.

During one of our strategy sessions, it was decided we would try to recruit members of the Black Stone Rangers (P Stone Nation) and the Gangster Disciples, two of the largest street gangs operating on the South Side. As coordinator of the Black Students for Defense, I believed the support of the gangs was essential. Coordination and security were not only needed for the success of the boycott but paramount to the general safety of the Black community and students.

I arranged a meeting with Jeff Fort, the leader of the Black P Stone Nation, at one of the Stone's headquarters in First Presbyterian Church in the Woodlawn area and headed by Reverend John Fry, a white Presbyterian clergyman.

I arrived at the church with two armed bodyguards and was greeted by Paul Martin (a.k.a. "Crazy Paul"), a member of the Main Twenty-One, the gang's governing body. The meeting, as I remember, was tense but respectful. Jeff said he agreed with our goals and the student movement even though he thought we should join the P Stone Nation. I declined, and he agreed to send representatives to the gang summit I was organizing at the Umoja Black Student Center.

The day of the meeting, Maséqua stood at the door and collected weapons from the gang members. Almost everybody was packing! During the summit, Maséqua was in the rafters with a shotgun guarding my back. The meeting went flawlessly, and several of the gang members joined our student movement efforts. Whenever I hear the term "she's got my back," I always think of Maséqua and how true the statement has been for me.

During my days as a leader in the Black student movement, I met Dr. Anderson Thompson. He was among a group of men who had come to support our movement. It was a time when powerful men committed to standing up with us to support our efforts and create much-needed change. Dr. Thompson, Dr. Bobby Wright, Harold Charles (Baba Hannibal Afrik), Cliff Washington, Lorenzo Martin, Alan Collard, and Dr. Harold Pates stand out as some of the brain trust that provided us with consultation, support, and strategy. It was also during this period that I had the opportunity to hear, meet, and work with Fred Hampton, Stokely Carmichael, Maulana Karenga (the founder of Kwanzaa), Amiri Baraka, John Hope Franklin, Michael X, Allan Collard, Tony Martin, Dr. Barbara Sizemore, Minister Louis Farrakhan, Rev. Jesse Jackson, and H. Rap Brown.

Following the massacre of Chairman Fred Hampton and Mark Clark; Maséqua, her father and I visited the Black Panther's apartment. The crime scene was overwhelming.

When Blackness was Golden

Bullet holes were everywhere, and the apartment was completely ransacked. The sight of all the blood, especially on the chairman's bed, was nauseating. Witnessing a scene like that will either make you want to fight or run and hide. It made me continue to find ways to fight injustice!

Sammy Davis Jr. was one of the secret supporters of the student movement; he donated $20,000 to support the Center and our boycott efforts. Sammy Davis (the Michael Jackson of his generation) was performing in Golden Boy in downtown Chicago, and I had the opportunity to visit him in his suite at the Conrad Hilton Hotel. It was my first time in a hotel's presidential suite, and it was amazing. He had a camera connected to some binoculars overlooking Grant Park. I also met my first celebrity entertainer, the beautiful Lola Falana, in the suite when she returned from a shopping spree. Sammy Davis Jr. was kind and concerned for the students when we informed him of our movement. He was also shorter than I imagined.

Members of our student organization were invited to the Auditorium Theatre to see Sammy Davis Jr. in Golden Boy. Maséqua got a ticket, but I didn't. Davis appeared in Golden Boy at the Auditorium for nearly a month. He portrayed Joe Wellington, a young Black man from Harlem who takes up prizefighting and ends up falling in love with his manager's girlfriend, Lorna, a White woman.

The boycotts continued for six Mondays, and even though all our demands were not met, The Board of Education met enough of them for us to stop the boycotts and return to our schools feeling victorious!

Following the boycotts, I was invited to represent the Afro-American Student Organization and speak on a program in New York with H. Rap Brown and Stokely Carmichael. Jim Harvey told me I couldn't go because I didn't speak well enough. Years later, while moderating a panel at the DuSable Museum of African American History, I thanked Jim for his negative critique because it gave me the motivation to never be told I didn't speak well enough again. Since that day in 1969, I have spoken on many occasions around the world!

Eyes and spies were everywhere!

Artwork by my brother Harold Ray, 2013

When Blackness was Golden

The following pages are from the FBI files collected on our student activities by the Subversive Activities Control Board, which was active from 1942 to 1972.

AFRO-AMERICAN STUDENT ASSOCIATION INFLUENCE:

On 13 October 1968, the Afro-American Student Association emerged as the central organization behind the boycott. At a meeting held at its headquarters attended by representatives of thirteen (13) Chicago High Schools, the group in essence consolidated all the different demands of the various groups from the various schools into a single list of twelve (12) demands that would be supported by all the students groups. At a press conference following the meeting, Victor Adams, Hubbard Jones, and Anthony Ray made these demands known. This list of demands (Appendix H) was to be presented to School Superindent James Redmond on 14 October 1968. They further called for a city-wide boycott of the high schools on 14 October 1968 asking other students sympathetic to their cause to join in. All students participating in the boycott were invited to a rally at the Afro-Arts Theater, 3947 S. Drexel, at 12:00 noon. During the press conference, Ray stated that if Redmond did not respond to their demands by Wednesday, 16 October 1968, .."we will cut the school week to four days, and we will teach ourselves on the fifth day" indicating that the boycotts would become a weekly occurance.

163641

Intelligence Division - B.I.S.   28 October 1968

ANALYTICAL REPORT

EVENT:
   Student Boycott of Chicago Schools

DATES:
   16 September 1968 to present and continuing.

PLACE:
   Numerous Chicago Public High Schools

PURPOSE:
   To secure concessions from the Board of Education to a list of demands concerning more recognition for negroes and more negroes in administrative positions in predominatly negro high schools.

SPONSORING ORGANIZATION:
   <u>Afro-American Students Association also known as Concerned Black Students</u> (a militant black nationalist organization with headquarters at 251 E. 39th Street).

AFFILIATED ORGANIZATIONS:
   <u>The New Breed</u> (Afro-American student group at Harrison High School), <u>Black Students for Defense</u> (The local subdivision of the Afro-American Students Association located at the individual high schools) and the <u>Latin American Action Committee</u> (Latin American student group at Harrison High School and Latin American counterpart to the New Breed.

163634

-1-

CONFIDENTIAL

When Blackness was Golden

#1086 General Schools

INTELLIGENCE DIVISION	CHICAGO POLICE DEPARTMENT

SURVEILLANCE REPORT

DATE OF SURVEILLANCE: 30 Oct 1968
DATE OF REPORT: 31 Oct 1968
SUBJECT MATTER OF INVESTIGATION: BOARD OF EDUCATION MEETING WITH BOYCOTTING STUDENTS
TYPE OF SURVEILLANCE: Fixed
INVESTIGATORS: [redacted]

PURPOSE OF SURVEILLANCE
To identify participants, observe proceeding and obtain any other pertinent information relative to the SUBJECT.

TIME	OBSERVATION
5:30 P.M	Investigators arrived at the Board of Education Building, 228 N. La Salle St. and took up position inside the lobby for observation.
5:50 P.M	Observed JAMES HARVEY, PEMON RAMI and a group of five (5) other unidentified M/N arrive at the Board of Education.
6:05 P.M	Took a position inside the hearing room of the Board of Education and the meeting was shortly thereafter called to order by the Board President and Chairman FRANK WHISTON. The roll was called with nine members presnet and two absent.

Just prior to the commencing of the meeting, the black students called a cacaus with James Harvey. When the meeting began, the students that had been invited were called to speak and the majority of the Black Students that had been invited and were present refused to go forward and speak when their names were called.

The following students representatives from schools indicated did speak, however, all advocating support of the boycott, in varying degrees, some qualifying their reasons for their support and others being blunt, militant and very short in their comment, indicating their refusal to further comment because they felt that the proper boycott leaders had not been invited to attend the meeting:

VICTOR ADAMS - Harrison High School
GUILLERMO ALVARADO - Wells High School
ORA FERGUSON - DuSable High School
(Continued)

CONFIDENTIAL

SUPPORTING ORGANIZATIONS:

The following organizations have stated a position of support for the boycotting students: Operation Breadbasket (Economic Arm of the Southern Christian Leadership Conference), The Woodlawn Organization (Grass roots civil rights organization leaning towards militant action), Chicago Urban League (Grass roots civil rights organization), Latin American Ministerial Association (A group of clergymen organized by the Archbishop to protect the rights and further the cause of Spanish minority groups), Inner-City Principals Club (A recently formed group of old line liberals and frightened white school principals who express black support in an effort to prevent uprisings in their school districts), Teachers for Radical Change (An organization of mostly young white teachers in inner-city schools), Latin American Defense Organization (Militant Spanish civil rights organization), Spanish Action Committee (Semi-militant Spanish civil rights organization) and various local groups comprised mainly of the students' parents formed in support of the boycotting students, i.e., Concerned Parents of Harrison, Concerned People of Lawndale, Concerned People of Garfield, Morgan Park Planning Association, etc.

CONFIDENTIAL

APPENDIX I
PAMPHLETS DISTRIBUTED AT VARIOUS HIGH SCHOOLS
ANNOUNCING BOYCOTT OF 21 OCTOBER 1968

163685

CONFIDENTIAL

FACTS

Over 500 Hundred Years Our Black Brothers and Sisters have been mistreated and use by the whites! They say Black Student Don't need Anything they Don't know how to keep them But How would they know if We Never Had them to use. Black Brother's & Sister's Don't Be No Fool Don't come to School Monday Oct. 21, 1968 Wake Up Get

CONFIDENTIAL

NO! SCHOOL MONDAY

MONDAY OCT. 21
34,000 BLACK STUDENTS STAYED HOME!
800 BLACK TEACHERS STAYED HOME!

COMMUNITY SUPPORT COMES TO STUDENTS FROM ALL ACROSS CHICAGO

COLLEGE STUDENTS MARCH IN SUPPORT!

WE WILL WIN!

(side margin: DOWN! FEAR DOPE THREATS CALL 624-1588)

(side margin: BOYCOTT STILL ON)

163691

The FBI files were made available to me by professor and educational historian Dionne Danns who discovered them while doing research for her dissertation, "Something Better for our Children: Black Organizing in Chicago Public Schools 1963–1971." I'm thankful Dionne located the FBI files since they kept better records than we did!

When Blackness was Golden

As beautiful as the '60s were culturally, they were also rife with racism, deaths, people going to jail, and overall fear of the future. The deaths of Malcolm X, Dr. King, and so many others left us wondering will any approach we use make a difference in the minds of the children of former slave masters and colonizers? Some people simply lost hope or got trapped in the drug war waged against the Black community or disappeared into corporate America or academia. But a lot of us didn't give up; we just shifted our directions and intention to social justice, arts, and politics to see if that could make a difference. The elections of Mayor Hatcher in Gary, Indiana; Mayor Carl Stokes in Cleveland, Ohio; and Mayor Coleman Young in Detroit, Michigan, were signs of hope and unity. But in the meantime, we lost a generation of warriors and leaders to jail, drugs, or death.

Moving Forward

African Proverb - Father to Son

> "Daddy, you tell me that the lion is the king of the jungle; yet in every book I read, the man always kills the lion! Father, why is that so?" The father looked at his son and said, "Until the lion learns to write, the story will always end the same."

When I heard H. Rap Brown relate this version of an African proverb those long years ago, it became the foundation for my cultural nationalism philosophy. Simply put, we must tell our own story or others will define us—and not necessarily in the proper light.

Continuing my move toward independence at nineteen, I bought a car (1969 Sunbeam Alpine) and moved from Stateway Gardens into my own place, a garden apartment on Eightieth and Ellis. I took all types of jobs to finance my independence, from short-order cook to washing dishes and pots in restaurants just long enough to get money to put on a show.

Bird of the Iron Feather

In 1970, I was cast as an actor in America's first Black soap opera, *Bird of the Iron Feather,* which aired on WTTW when it was known as National Educational Television before being rebranded as Public Broadcasting Service (PBS). *Bird of the Iron Feather* was a TV show by Black people for Black people. The scripts were written around things that happened in Black people's daily lives.

The protagonist was a Black detective who was killed in a riot, and the story was seen through flashbacks from his diary. Jonah, at thirty-five, was the patriarch of a family of thirteen, including his gang member and dropout brother, his militant sister, two deaf mutes, and his aunt and uncle, who were welfare recipients. In the beginning, Jonah tried to work within the system but became increasingly militant as the series developed. Bird was the highest-rated local production in the WTTW station's history. The series was picked up by other PBS stations across the country.

The station's original plan was to hire two white directors and for the scripts to be written by white students. When the Coalition for United Community Action—headed by the Reverend C. T. Vivian and Richard Durham, an award-winning investigative reporter and writer for the Chicago Defender and Muhammad Speaks—learned of the plan, they challenged it.

When Blackness was Golden

In 1969, there were no Black television directors in Chicago. Richard Durham informed Okoro Harold Johnson, an accomplished theatre director, about a six-week director training program being offered at WGBH TV station in Boston. Okoro decided to attend, and he received a certificate. Johnson returned to Chicago and was hired to direct several episodes. The episodes I appeared in were directed by Okoro and the other Black director, Roy Inman. Bird was written and created by famed writer Richard Durham. Clarence McIntosh was executive producer, and the theme song was written and performed by Oscar Brown Jr.

A scene from *Bird of the Iron Feather,* episode "His-Story and Mine"

Episodes aired three times a week. Prior to Bird, Richard Durham also created the *"Destination Freedom"* radio program. During the 1960s, he was the editor of Muhammad Speaks and served as the credited ghostwriter of Muhammad Ali's 1975 autobiography, *The Greatest: My Own Story.* Bird featured several local Black talents in front of the camera and premiered in January 1970 and was funded by a $600,000 grant from the Ford Foundation for thirty-five episodes. The station was accused of misusing the funds, and only twenty-one episodes were produced. When I watched the show on television, I felt the actors that were training with me gave much better performances than I did, so I gave up acting and focused on directing and teaching. Only three known episodes still exist. WTTW claimed the other episodes were taped over sometime after airing.

Following Bird of the Iron Feather

One of the benefits of working on a pioneering television show was the opportunity to be exposed to so many incredibly talented people that were introduced to working behind the scenes in the early '70s. During that time, very few opportunities were available for Black people to work in television in front of or behind the camera. Many of the actors and directors were working in theatre due to the lack of opportunity to break into television. My exposure to Bird gave me the opportunity to dream and to see myself in a position where I could create television, theatre, and film projects.

Maséqua and I developed a music video for the Arizona Department of Education titled, *"Follow Your Dream."* The chorus for that song was, "First you have to see it and then you can be it!" It is a fact that you must be in a position where you can see a future that is promising so that it gives you the motivation to go to the top of the mountain or at least be motivated to try.

Living on the South Side of Chicago, specifically on Thirty-Ninth Street, and going to WTTW on the Northwest Side at 5400 North Saint Louis took me approximately two hours on public transportation. But the distance and travel time didn't trouble me because I had a reoccurring role on a new TV show!

Bird of the Iron Feather premiered in January 1970 and became a huge ratings success for WTTW and other PBS stations around the country. When I sat in my mother and father's living room watching the show, I was moved by the amount of incredible Black talent from Chicago represented on television for the first time. A bonus was my longtime mentor Okoro Harold Johnson becoming one of the series directors. Getting an opportunity to watch him transition from theatre to television was amazing. Okoro, in many ways, represented what I wanted to become.

Bird of the Iron Feather helped me decide to change my focus from acting to directing. Once I made that decision, I realized I could not just direct because I would have to wait around for people to give me an opportunity. It became clear that I needed to produce as well, so that's what I did. I took any job I could get to pursue my dream. I worked as a short-order cook, pot washer, dishwasher, waiter—anything that would allow me to generate enough money to rent theatres and pay for costumes and props. I would go to the print shop in the basement at Wendell Phillips High School to print my tickets, flyers, and posters with the support and assistance of Mr. Pfister, the print shop teacher. I continue to design the graphic material for many of my productions.

When Bird ended, I started looking for a new job opportunity. I went to my mother, who was part of Richard J. Daley's democratic machine. She was a precinct captain and worked the polls on election days getting people out to vote. Every year, a major fundraising party was held at the armory on Fifty-Sixth Street and Cottage Grove. The precinct captains were responsible for selling tickets, purchasing a table, and providing alcohol for the attendees at their table. They had to sell a certain number of tickets or buy them.

My mom sent me to the ward boss, Edison Love, who wrote a letter of recommendation to the Chicago Park District. I was hired immediately! No interview, no resume required! It was an example of the patronage system of Chicago working at its best.

The democratic organization in Chicago controlled jobs and placed who they wanted where they wanted them. If you were of value to them, they would take care of you and your family. So, I got my first "real job" as drama instructor at Stateway Park where years before I had watched Okoro Harold Johnson teach! I had come full circle!

And then I was introduced to my next mentor, Theodore Ward.

Chapter Seven: Theodore Ward

> "Greatness should not be determined by name recognition but rather by contributions made and lives touched!"
>
> Pemon Rami

One day while playing basketball, a young artist named Russell Davis approached me and said he had someone I should meet. Russell was a friend of my brother Harold, and they had attended the Chicago School of the Art Institute together. Russell was also an aspiring actor. He took me to the Louis Theatre on Thirty-Fifth and Michigan to meet Theodore Ward, who was considered the godfather of Black theatre.

Ted was one of the first Black dramatists to win the Guggenheim Fellowship, which allowed him to move his career forward and publish thirty plays. Along with Richard Wright, Ted joined the Chicago Writers Workshop of the WPA Federal Theatre. When the WPA ended, he, along with Langston Hughes, Loften Mitchell, Paul Robeson, and Owen Dodson, founded and headed the Negro Playwrights Company. Ted's play about the Marcus Garvey Movement, *Big White Fog,* starred Canada Lee. It was the Workshop's first production.

In 1947, *Our Lan,* his play about the Reconstruction South, ran on Broadway for forty-two performances. The night I went to meet Ted, they were presenting *Our Lan* at the South Side Center for the Performing Arts, and I was once again blown away! I was at the theatre every day after that! Ted was sixty-five when he opened the South Side Center for the Performing Arts.

Ted Ward, the godfather of Black Theatre

The second play I attended at the South Side Center for the Performing Arts was *Slow Dance on the Killing Ground*, written by William Hanley and directed by Okoro Harold Johnson. The play focuses on a Black fugitive played skillfully by David McKnight. The other characters were an older German refugee and a white teenager on her way to an abortion when they converge in a Brooklyn neighborhood bar. My mind was blown by this incredible production. There was a scene with Randle bathed in red lights as he explains the hole in his heart and killing his mother that still haunts me to think about!

Ted became my mentor and talked to me constantly about his views on theatre, politics, and life as he took me under his wing. One of the outstanding actors at the theatre was Letitia "Tish" Toole, a mainstay at the theatre. Overhearing the debates between her and Ted about acting was invaluable!

When Blackness was Golden

Letitia starred in *A Son Come Home*, *No Use Crying*, and *Who's Got His Own* at the South Side Center for the Performing Arts.

The first play I performed in at the South Side Center for the Performing Arts was Ed Bullins' *How Do You Do*, directed by Leander Jones in 1968. My acting partner was Kim Sizemore, the daughter of famed educator Dr. Barbara Sizemore. When Kim left the play, an actress named Ivory Stone took over the role. Following a few performances, Ivory informed the cast she was leaving the show to go on tour with Smokey Robinson as a background singer (and rumored girlfriend). Ted planned to cancel the production until Maséqua, who had been volunteering at the theatre and working the box office, informed us she knew the lines and could play the part of the streetwalker. She had watched every performance and knew all the blocking and lines. Ted couldn't fathom her doing the role, but when she read for it, he was impressed. She stepped right in, and the show went on.

During the year I spent with Ted, I also was an actor in productions of *The Electronic Nigger* and *A Son Come Home*.

My first directing opportunity at South Side Center for the Performing Arts was Ron Milner's play, *The Monster*, which I staged in 1969. I cast Paul Butler in his first play in the lead role of *The Monster*.

With Paul Butler at the Goodman Theatre

Maséqua's brother, Raybon, was a member of the cast, and her brother, Relman, was the lighting operator. The play focused on the developing Black political leadership.

Paul Butler went on to become a star of stage and screens and won universal acclaim for his creation of the role of Becker in August Wilson's *Jitney*. He played Antony to Vanessa Redgrave's *Cleopatra in London*, and Shylock in Peter Sellars' production of *The Merchant of Venice* at the Goodman Theatre and in London, Paris, and Hamburg. On Broadway, Paul created the role of Navy Captain Judge Randolph in *A Few Good Men*. He appeared in numerous shows at the Goodman Theatre, including *Death and the King's Horsemen* at the Kennedy Center and *Jitney*. On film, Paul's credits include, *The Insider, Strictly Business, Glengarry Glen Ross, To Sleep with Anger,* and *The Spook Who Sat by the Door*.

During the production of *The Monster*, Paul's career almost ended abruptly. For the play, I had rigged a way to hang

Paul's character. We built a long table which we placed behind a curtain so the audience couldn't see the table legs. Paul would stand on a milk crate which was kicked from under his legs, and his butt would catch the end of the table so his feet could dangle while he was simulating hanging. During a performance, he slipped off the edge of the table and was hanging for real until he could wiggle his way back up on the table. After the show, I told him how incredible his performance was, and he informed me he was actually hanging for real! My first close call!

Scene from the production of *The Monster* I directed at the South Side Center for the Performing Arts in 1969

Theodore Ward wrote more than thirty plays as well as essays, poetry, and the libretto for two folk operas. One of his libretti, *Our Lan*, was the first play I saw at the theatre. *Our Lan* first premiered on Broadway at New York's Royale Theatre in 1947. Set in the closing moment after the Civil War, the play comprises two stories. The first is that of a community of recently emancipated freedmen who settled on an island plantation off the Georgia coast given to them by General Sherman's order as part of post-war land reforms. Their struggle to make the land prosper and a betrayal by the government sets the scene for a second story.

The second story focused on the central character, Joshuah Tain, a "humble but charismatic leader" who emerges among the freedmen. The theatre had 500 seats, and for most performances there were more actors on stage than in the audience. Ted persevered as long as he could and finally shut the doors in 1972. When the theatre closed, I formed another theatrical performing group as the umbrella for our productions and classes. We named it Independent Professional Performing Artists (IPPA).

Ted was my theatre father, and he came to support every show I directed in the '70s. The City of Chicago proclaimed April 23, 1977, Theodore Ward Day. Ted passed away May 8, 1983.

A Bite Out of the Big Apple

One of the plays Ted produced at the South Side Center for the Performing Arts was *A Son Come Home*, written by Ed Bullins. A line from the play stated, "Two hours down the Jersey Turnpike, the trip beginning at the New York Port Authority terminal, then straight down through New Jersey to Philadelphia and home." I remembered those lines when I traveled to visit my sister Barbara in Philly. I took the two-hour bus ride to New York. When I arrived at the Port Authority terminal, I looked up at the skyscrapers and said, "Wow, the Big Apple!" When I looked back down, I saw Oscar Brown Jr. and Muhammad Ali walking down the street. Oscar and his wife, Jean Pace, had staged the Broadway production of *Big Time Buck White*, starring Ali. At nineteen years old, I had the opportunity to spend time with them backstage at the theatre as well as in Muhammad's hotel suite, which was always filled with beautiful women. I had a ball just watching the goings and comings, including the unexpected arrival of Muhammad's wife at the time!

The play centered on Big Time Buck White (played by Ali), a militant Black leader who addresses a meeting organized by a Black political group. Oscar adapted the musical from Joseph Dolan Tuotti's play, also titled, *Big Time Buck White*.

The closing monologue, delivered by the character Big Time and written by Oscar, still lives with me today.

> "We are joined in the struggle of each new generation
> It is an age-old faithful confrontation
> On which the one hand, the oppressor stands.
> The military law and order band
> Recruiting their spies, relying on lies
> Looting, shooting, beating, cheating
> the human race of its richest resources.
> Diverting mankind from nobler courses
> With well-established forces of deceit and defeat,
> There on one hand they hold the land
> While here on the other rise those who cry brother
> And love one another
> Who suffer to reach and to teach and to preach
> a different style of living far more giving and kind."

Spending time backstage and in the audience of *Big Time Buck White* was the beginning of my numerous visits to New York to see plays and take classes. Ted Ward had told me that if I wanted to be great, I had to learn from greats!

My studies in New York began with an invitation from Ernie McClintock, director, acting teacher, and producer of the Afro-American Studio for Acting & Speech in Harlem. Ernie was originally from Chicago. During my visit, his production of N. R. Davidson's *El Hajj Malik* was being performed at the theatre.

El Hajj Malik was a groundbreaking play about the life and impact of Malcolm X. The play left an indelible impression on me. Ernie founded three institutions in Harlem: the Afro-American Studio for Acting & Speech (1966), the 127th Street Repertory Ensemble (1973), and the Jazz Theatre of Harlem (1986).

My next training stop in New York was at Dr. Barbara Ann Teer's National Black Theatre. In the 1960s, Teer began teaching drama at Harlem's Wadleigh Junior High School, and her methods became the foundation for the world-renowned Negro Ensemble Company.

Dr. Teer was an award-winning performer, director, visionary entrepreneur, and champion of the Black Arts Movement. National Black Theatre generated a new way of releasing the soul energy inherent in the Black lifestyle called "The Five Cycles of Evolution" to move participants from "self-conscious art to god-conscious art." I was also impressed with their facility on 125th Street. The production I attended started on a street setting with all the standard street characters for the first half of the show. At intermission the walls opened, and the setting became a temple. Wow! Aside from acting, their workshops included: evolutionary movement/dance, meditation, spiritual release, liberation theory, numerology, astrology, and ideology.

During my days in New York, I also had the chance to meet and get to know Ashton Springer, the Broadway producer whose credits included *Bubbling Brown Sugar* and *Eubie* the Musical; Garland Cain of the Last Poets; actor Gilbert Lewis; Robert Macbeth, founder and director of the New Lafayette Theatre; writer Paul Carter Harrison; Obba Babatunde; Woody King; and Whitman Mayo.

Following my incredible time of study and introspection in New York, I returned to Chicago to continue my quest to become a great director and producer.

On August 31, 1970, Maséqua gave birth to our first son, Babatunde Olugbala, at Garfield Park Hospital. The name Babatunde means 'grandfather returns' in Yoruba. Olugbala means the savior of our people. A lot of pressure for a young man! Babatunde's naming ceremony was officiated by Dr. Anderson Thompson and Kelan Phil Cohran played his harp. It would be a few more years before we got married.

Chapter Eight: Lights up on Black Theatre

"Talent is developed as a result of opportunity."
Pemon Rami

To discuss contemporary Black theatre, especially in Chicago, we must start with the Pekin Theatre, which was located at Twenty-Seventh and State. The Pekin was the first Black-owned musical and vaudeville stock theatre in the United States. Founded by Robert T. Motts in 1905, the theatre served as a training ground and showcase for Black theatrical talent, vaudeville acts, and musical comedies.

The Regal Theatre opened in February 1928 and, over the decades, featured some of the greatest entertainers of the time. The Regal featured both motion pictures and live stage shows. Nat "King" Cole, Cab Calloway, Louis Armstrong, Ella Fitzgerald, Sarah Vaughan, Lena Horne, Dinah Washington, Miles Davis, Sammy Davis Jr., Lionel Hampton, Dizzy Gillespie, and Duke Ellington were a few of the performers. Imagine seeing these greats in your neighborhood theatre along with the Jackson Five, the Five Stairsteps, and Smokey Robinson and the Miracles as I had the opportunity to do.

Often compared to Harlem's Apollo Theatre, the Chicago historic Regal Theatre, at 4719 South Parkway (now known as Dr. Martin Luther King Jr. Drive), was down the street from the famous Savoy Ballroom and the South Center department store. The South Center department store catered almost exclusively to the Black community. An entire floor of the store was used as the training ground for Madame C. J. Walker, a beauty school which helped men and women become independent business owners. For four decades, until 1968, the 3,000-seat Regal guaranteed the very best in African-American entertainment.

When Blackness was Golden

In 1933, Theodore Ward became the recreation director for the Abraham Lincoln Centre and taught speech and dramatic writing. Ted eventually was hired in a position with the Negro Unit of Chicago's branch of the Federal Theatre Project along with Richard Wright, author of the novel Native Son.

In 1935 President Franklin D. Roosevelt established the Federal Theatre Project (1935-1939) as part of the New Deal, a series of domestic programs (lasting roughly from 1933 to 1939) implemented to combat the effects of the Great Depression. It was an economic recovery project similar to what the nation is going through today with the COVID-19 economic recovery. The Negro Theatre Project (NTP) grew out of this in twenty-three cities, one of which was Chicago. Shirley Graham (who later married W. E. B. DuBois) gave leadership to the Chicago NTP.

In 1938, Fanny McConnell Ellison became Executive Director of the Chicago Negro People's Theatre, housed at Good Shepherd Community Theatre and eventually re-named Parkway Community House at 500 East Sixty-Seventh Street. Mrs. Ellison later worked for the Chicago Defender, where she wrote a column called "Along the Political Front" as well as reviews and essays.
The 1940s were the beginning of Chicago's first Black theatre renaissance. Langston Hughes founded the Skyloft Players at the Parkway Community House. The Federal Theatre was formed by Ted Ward and Richard Wright. Chicago Negro Theatre was created by Margaret Goss Burroughs. The DuBois Theatre Guild was formed by Oscar Brown Jr., Richard Durham, and Vernon Jarrett. The Tempo Players was started by Walter Lott and the Newer Still Players by John Houston.

Val Gray Ward and the Kuumba Workshop

When Val Gray Ward entered a room, the first thing you noticed was her powerful and emotional voice. The actress, producer, cultural vanguard, and internationally known dramatist was born Q. Valeria Ward on August 21, 1932, in Mound Bayou, Mississippi, one of the oldest all-Black towns in America.

Val moved to Chicago in 1951 where she got married and mothered five children while becoming active in Chicago's African-American cultural activities. She developed friendships in Chicago with Dr. Margaret Burroughs, Gwendolyn Brooks, Hoyt Fuller, Haki R. Madhubuti, and Abena Joan Brown, to name a few.

In 1968, she and Francis formed the Kuumba Theatre. Kuumba (which means clean-up, create, and build in Kiswahili) was dedicated to the revitalization of the Black community through the arts. Under Val's direction, Kuumba became internationally recognized as one of America's leading Black theatre companies.

I first experienced a Val Gray Ward performance at A. J. Williams' bookstore, at 652 E. Seventy-Ninth Street in Chicago. In the back of the store was a performance space. A. J. would have artists come in to perform, and Maséqua, her mother, and I attended. Val Gray performed *"Between the World and Me"* by Richard Wright. I had never in my life seen anything like it. The passion, pain, and anger demonstrated in her performance was overwhelming! When she gets to the end of the poem about the dry bones, you know you were in the grave with this person.

Val became the voice of Black poetry! Her dramatizations of poems made people understand and feel the material in ways that few writers could do themselves. Val was, by far, the person who could creatively demonstrate and define the purpose and objectives of the Chicago Black Arts Movement. Val Gray Ward's definition for something to be classified as Black art was that it had to be "by, for, and about Black people!" If a creative piece of work was going to be philosophically defined as a Black Theatre piece, it was going to be written by a Black person, for a Black audience, and it had to be a story about Black people.

So, that context had a great deal to do with the kind of material that Kuumba presented, and it gave specific directions to what was expected of actors, writers, directors, and craftspeople when they came there to work. The experiences Val and Francis created in the theatre were revolutionary at the time. All performances opened with a ritual and closed with one as well.

The ritual was a combination of blues, gospel, dramatic sounds, and poetry that set the mood for what the audience should expect, and it was all done in the dark theatre.

Kuumba Ritual

> Kuumba create is a school for living survival
> For living Blackness
> Black artists creating to, for, from our people
> To, for, from Black people
> Us
> We dancers, singers, writers, musicians, Black arts people
> creating from to us
> We, for living, for life, survival!

The audiences were exposed to a visceral cathartic cleansing at the beginning of each Kuumba production. There was a set of different standards for Kuumba performances which were unique from other theatre companies, including mine.

Kuumba integrated the seven principles of the Nguzu Saba in their performances. The Nguzu Saba is the seven basic values of African culture, which in English means the seven principles. The principles are: Umoja (Unity), Kujichagulia (Self-determination), Ujima (Collective Work and Responsibility), Ujamaa (Cooperative Economics), Nia (Purpose), Kuumba (Creativity), and Imani (Faith). Kuumba made a conscious effort to contribute ten percent of all the money they earned to other struggling Black cultural institutions.

Black organizations, including the South Side Community Art Center, the Institute of the Black World, and the DuSable Museum of African American History, were recipients of Kuumba's contributions. Kuumba presented some of its earlier theatre productions at the South Side Community Art Center and in return gave back to the organization even after moving on to its new location at 2222 South Michigan.

With Val Gray Ward and Wole Soyinka

I don't know of any other cultural institution doing that at that time. Val was one of those people who was instrumental in getting people to understand that you just can't get lost in your own world of creating. You've got to help the other

When Blackness was Golden

entities that are being created to go on. I became involved with Kuumba when I attended their workshop being held at the Black Women's Committee on Oakenwald Boulevard.

My first production with Kuumba was as an actor in a production titled *Unity and Destruction* at the University of Nebraska. The production was well-received, but when we returned to the airport for our flight back to Chicago, it was a different story!

One of the male dancers in the show broke his sandal and walked into the airport with no shoes on. The agent at the gate said he could only get on the plane if he looked, acted, and smelled normal and refused to let him on. When the cast members, led by Val, protested loudly at the gate, the airline finally relented and agreed to let the dancer board, and it was back to Chicago.

When Val Gray Ward became the director of the African American Cultural Center at Southern Illinois University in 1969, she asked me to become the interim director of Kuumba until she returned. Teaching acting, directing plays, and working with Kuumba's talented actors and staff was an extraordinary experience.

During my time at Kuumba, I was introduced to the poem *"Note on Commercial Theatre"* by famed poet Langston Hughes. Langston had relocated to Hollywood to pursue work in the film industry in 1935. His failure to find work in the lucrative movie trade was hampered by discrimination and racism. Langston returned to Chicago in 1941 and founded the Skyloft Players.

"Note on Commercial Theatre" was inspired by Langston's experiences in Los Angeles. The last verse of the poem reflects Val's life and commitment.

> "Someday somebody'll
> Stand up and talk about me,
> And write about me —
> Black and beautiful —
> And sing about me,
> And put on plays about me!
> I reckon it'll be
> Me myself!
> Yes, it'll be me."

The Black community was under attack from all sides. Infiltrators, police brutality, racial discrimination, constant surveillance, restrictive covenant, redlining, tenement housing, and poor schools are just a few examples of what we were up against.

In 1968 Hoover's FBI Targeted Black-Owned Bookstores

In a one-page directive, J. Edgar Hoover noted with alarm a recent increase in the establishment of Black extremist bookstores, which he believed represented propaganda outlets for revolutionary and hate publications and culture centers for extremism. As director of the Federal Bureau of Investigation, Hoover ordered each bureau office to "locate and identify Black extremist and/or African-type bookstores in its territory and open separate discreet investigations on each to determine if it is extremist in nature." Each investigation was to determine the identities of the owners; whether it is a front for any group or foreign interest; whether individuals affiliated with the store engage in extremist activities; the number, type, and source of books and material on sale; the store's financial condition; its clientele; and whether it is used as a headquarters or meeting place."

Published in The Atlantic by Joshua Clark Davis
February 19, 2018

My brothers Harold and Barry and me in a scene from the play *Old Judge Mose is Dead* by Joseph White in 1972

1969 and 1970 were important in my continued theatre evolution. I participated in numerous productions as an actor and director and taught acting classes in my home, at the Southside Community Art Center, the Parkway Community House, Hull House theatre, UNIA headquarters, and Abraham Lincoln Center. I also directed productions at Howard University, Olive-Harvey College, and Malcolm X College and tours of Chicago parks, high schools, libraries, and elementary schools.

In 1971, thanks to Karim Childs, then executive director of the Parkway Community House, I was permitted to use the facility to teach acting classes twice a week. In those days I didn't charge for classes because I was trying to build a theatre movement, and for that I needed to develop new talent. Later that year, I was informed that a new theatre group—the Experimental Black Actors Guild (X-BAG) founded by Clarence Taylor, Claudia McCormick, and Jean Davidson—was going to become the resident theatre company in the building, and I would no longer have access to teach classes. I was disappointed about losing the use of the theatre and excited at the same time for a new Black theatre to be opening.

I returned to touring productions and teaching acting. The United Negro Improvement Association honorable president, General Dr. Charles L. James, allowed me access to the UNIA headquarters for our classes and rehearsals. In 1940, Brother James was elected first vice president and co-founder of UNIA Division #401 in Chicago.

I also taught communication skills at the Opportunities Industrialization Center (OIC), a nonprofit adult education and job training organization headquartered in Philadelphia, Pennsylvania, established by Rev. Leon Sullivan. OIC operated in twenty-two states in the US, including Chicago, Illinois. While working there, I met a young man named Douglas Alan Mann, who was the butcher at a local market. Douglas explained he wanted to be an actor and asked if I had any advice. Because I wasn't in production at that time, I suggested he visit X-BAG and meet Clarence Taylor, which led to Doug's incredible acting, directing, and producing career.

Robert Townsend and The Experimental Black Actors Guild

The year 1974 was a very busy one for me. I converted *The Black Fairy*, the play written by Eugene Perkins, into a musical which I directed at the LaMont Zeno Theatre. I also directed *Where is the Pride What is the Joy* by Shirley Hardy at X-BAG. The theatre's director, Clarence Taylor, asked me to direct their opening production for their 1974 season, and

When Blackness was Golden

I readily agreed. After auditioning for over four hours, I was leaving the theatre and heard someone doing character voices like Humphrey Bogart, Alfred Hitchcock, and James Cagney for other actors that had auditioned. I asked the actor why he had not shown any of those skills during the audition. The seventeen-year-old actor's name was Robert Townsend.

Robert did an unimpressive audition, but after seeing his immense talent, I cast him in the play in a non-speaking role as a drug dealer who used the laundromat to dry out his weed. Robert stole the scene every time he came on stage. My accidentally hearing his character voices began our long history of working together. Robert's versatility as an actor allowed me to think differently about the productions I could produce.

When Harold Lee Rush left the cast of *Black Fairy*, it opened the door for Robert to replace him in the production. Townsend played multiple characters, including Aesop, Mr. Sun, Brer Rabbit, and the Signifying Monkey. His ability to create character voices added creativity and versatility to the show.

In our production of Wole Soyinka's *The Strong Breed*, directed by Maséqua, Robert played the eighty-year-old village elder. *The Strong Breed* was the first African play produced in Chicago. I also cast him in a small part in the 1975 films *Cooley High*, *The Monkey Hustle*, and *Mahogany*. Robert was a creative sponge, soaking up everything he saw and heard as he prepared to "break-out" of the limitation in front of him. He saw the possibilities and believed in himself. I often say to be a successful artist, you must have the audacity to believe in yourself and what you are doing. All the naysayers be damned!

I also cast Robert in his first national commercial for Pepsi. When he subsequently transferred to William Patterson College in New Jersey, I traveled to the college to assist him in directing his first play. Townsend's mother, Shirley, and his siblings came to the Zeno theatre often to see his performances and were very supportive of his dreams. I would visit Robert often when I traveled to New York, and I would hang out at the comedy clubs where he was honing his stand-up act. He was hilarious even back then, but he also was beginning to understand the importance of creating his own path and defining his own aesthetic. I have been very proud to see his development and influence on American culture and the entertainment industry.

The LaMont Zeno Theatre

In June 1973, I was asked to take a job establishing a theatre at the Better Boys Foundation (BBF) on Chicago's West Side. At the same time, I'd been cast in *The Spook Who Sat by the Door* and was leaving for Hollywood to film my scenes. I decided to hold off on my decision about the job until I returned to Chicago.

When I returned from California, I was told that BBF's executive staff had been killed in an airplane crash. Edison Hoard, president of the board, and staff members Lamont Zeno, Bill Smith, and Rita Cody were traveling by plane to visit a summer camp for BBF members. I seriously contemplated whether to take the job because of the gloom that was hanging over the institution. I eventually decided to take the five dollars per hour part-time job and went about the business of building the theatre.

"At that time, there weren't many Black theatre facilities in Chicago. So, philosophically, I created a theatre that was by, for, and about Black people. And I designed it programmatically in a way to be uplifting — in a way that we would win." The BBF board of directors wanted to name the theatre after Smith, Cody, Zeno, and Hoard. I lobbied for it to be named for Lamont Zeno, the BBF program director who was instrumental in establishing the idea for the theatre. They eventually agreed. From conception to construction, I built the stage, installed lighting, and did everything we needed to have a real theatre.

"I saw that the camera could be a weapon against poverty, against racism, against all sorts of social wrongs. I knew at that point I had to have a camera."

Gordon Parks

Picture of me taken outside of the Umoja Black Student Center by Bobby Crawford in 1968

When Blackness was Golden

My grandmother Savannah's father Charlie Paramore and mother Silva Cunningham

Oscar Ray and Savannah Paramore, my paternal grandfather and grandmother

My maternal grandfather and Pullman Porter Dewey Foster

I was born
August 9, 1950

My family attending opening night at the production of *"The Wiz"* which I directed at Kalamazoo Civic Theatre in Kalamazoo, Michigan

Hanging out with my sons Babatunde and Tacuma in Las Vegas

When Blackness was Golden

In 1975 I produced the *Black Fairy* album based on a play by Useni Eugene Perkins that I converted to a musical. We recorded the album at the late Paul Serrano's, P.S. Recording Studios.

I assembled great musicians such as the amazing Chico Freeman, Anthony Llorens and Jerry "Jami" Johnson to support the incredible singers from the original cast of the play. I must mention Patricia Crawford as the Black Fairy; Maséqua Myers as the Queen Mother; Denise Llorens as Black Bird; Barry Ray as Uncle Remus and the vocals of Gregory Curry.

The song *"Black Land of the Nile"* was reissued in 2006 by Jazzman records in London in and became an instant hit.

The song with lead vocals by Maséqua tells of the splendors of Egypt and suggests to the listener that its heritage is more a part of Africa than the Middle East as it is generally thought today. The message is as relevant and poignant today as when we recorded it over 48 years ago.

"Of Boys and Men" was selected as the Centerpiece film at the 16th Pan African Film festival held at the Magic Johnson Theatre in Los Angeles

"Of Boys and Men" also premiered at the Chicago International Film Festival

USA | 2012 | 28 min.
Director: Masequa Myers
Genre: Documentary
English

Thursday, April 18, 2013, 8:45 pm
& Thursday, April 25, 2013, 6:00 pm
AMC Loews Theatres
600 N. Michigan Ave.
Chicago, IL 60611

Shown with Peru Sabe.
Cuisine as an Agent of Social Change

This is the story of a family's love and tragic loss of their only child while residing in Chicago's Pilsen Community. It centers on Jeff Abbey Maldonado, Jr. an aspiring hip hop artist, known as J-DEF, who was determined to use his talent and creativity to make a positive change in his community and in society.

I met Spike Lee on numerous occasions including at his store on Sunset Boulevard in Los Angeles. This is a picture from when he visited me at the DuSable Museum.

Bill Duke and D Channis Berry at the pre-release screening of the documentary, *Dark Girls*.

When Blackness was Golden

Hanging out with Gladys Knight following a rehearsal for the play I directed *Madame Lily*.

Nancy Wilson was incredible at a concert I produced with her in Los Angeles

I produced a concert with Stevie Wonder at the Vision Theatre in Los Angeles

A project Masequa and I produced in Los Angeles for actors in 2002

Maséqua and I were pleased to be featured on the cover of the *South Shore Current Magazine*. The photo was taken by Tony Smith. The publication was established by Yvette Moyo "to tell the truth about the people, the art, the culture and the countless human and natural resources in Chicago's South Shore community."

Something new in 'The Strong Breed'

Pemon Rami (left) and Berry Gordy

Billy Dee Williams rapping

Pemon Rami

Diana Ross relaxing

Diana Ross with a little friend

The Lamont Zeno Community Theatre of the Better Boys Foundation was bristling with excitement early this fall and into the winter months when members from the cast of "Mahogany" used its facilities for several scenes.

One can imagine how thrilled the youths were who enjoy activities at the Lamont Zeno Community Theatre and the facilities of the Better Boys Foundation.

Each day Diana Ross, billy Dee Williams, Berry Gordy and other principals in the movie felt at ease with the young people.

The Foundation doesn't need the celebrities to insure excitement or to bring enthusiasm because of its active program and in recent years the theatre program has proved vital to the development of youths, actors and adults.

One of the artistic behind this increased cultural activity is Pemon Rami, the producer and director of the theatre. Since he has been appointed to this position such productions as "Odu," "Slave Story," "Black Fairy," and "The Dozen" has been featured.

A traditional African drama by Wole Soyinka entitled "The Strong Breed" is the next feature and will be directed by Khouads "Mane'Qua" Myers.

Rami, who was formerly known as Anthony Ray before converting to his new identity, has developed into a very influential leader in the world of drama.

Following graduation from Carter and Attucks elementary school Rami became interested in theatre quite by accident. At first his artistic interest was centered in conga drums and percussion instruments and performed with the Exotica Conga Group. Incidentally, they were placed first in a Montgomery Ward contest, but was disqualified in the finals after placing 4th over 300 other groups. This experience discouraged him from considering music as a profession.

It was his desire to develop a skit for a production that increased his interest. Harold Johnson and James Hues helped him to develop his stage revue.

That was the beginning that led him to associations with the Independent Professional Performing Artist, Kuumba Workshop, Taifa Builders and the LaMont Zeno Community.

More recently he has been involved in movies such as "Three Tough Guys," "Up Town Saturday Night," "Spook Who Sat By The Door" as Shorty Duncan and served as casting director for "Mahogany."

Directing chores has taken Rami to the University of Nebraska for "Unity and Destruction," Haward University for "Valley of the Bones," "Nocturns on the Rhine" at the YWCA Hotel, "The Monster" as the Southside Center of Performing Arts, "On the Darker Side," at Dunbar High School, "Shades of Black Beauty," for a tour of the Chicago Park District, "Sister Sonji," YWCA Hotel, "We, the People, Darker Than Blue," at Olive Harvey College, "Mission Accomplished," at Lincoln Center, "Green all of Freedom" at Malcolm X College, "The Job" which toured elementary schools in Chicago, "Contribution" at Roosevelt University and "The Uncle Toms" at the Stateway Park District.

Rami who will be serving as producer for "The Strong Breed" thinks that Soyinka's drama will be the most challenging of all the plays he has produced.

"Strong Breed" will open for three weekends at the Better Boys Foundation April 4 through 20 with a curtain at 8 p.m. The Zeno Community Theatre is a member of the Black Theatre Alliance.

Earl Calloway

When Blackness was Golden

Creating Dynamic Media for Business

AV VIDEO MULTIMEDIA Producer

November 2002 Vol. 24/No. 11 $5.95

The 2002 Top 100 Producers
Winners of our 8th annual contest

● **MASEQUA MYERS-RAMI**

Company: Masequa Myers & Associates
Location: Los Angeles, CA   Age: 49
Title: founder and CEO
Applications: sales/marketing, training, presentation, education

"Passion drives me," says Myers-Rami, whose theatrical training and experience is at the core of a widely diverse career path that has included film development, television production, documentaries and multimedia design projects for theaters and medical institutions. Working since the '70s with her husband, Pemon, Myers-Rami opened her current company in 1992. "We contract projects and clients who aspire to be innovative in educating and entertaining simultaneously," says Myers-Rami. "The bulk of our work is highly diverse and focuses on consultation and production of promoting the correct image of a person and/or a business or their product." Recent projects have included producing an entertaining instructional video for teens, "Have a Healthy Baby," for the Maricopa County Health Department in Phoenix, Arizona, and a national radio talk show called "You Decide" for KPFK-FM in Los Angeles (and KLCA.com on the Web). "Because so many of our projects involve teaching and the youth population, I believe I'm making a strong contribution to the uplifting of America's future generations, and that makes me very proud," says Myers-Rami.

● **PEMON RAMI**

Company: Masequa Myers & Associates   Location: Los Angeles, CA
Age: 52   Title: chief technical officer
Applications: sales/marketing, training, presentation, education

Rami, who has partnered in business with his wife, Masequa Myers, for more than 20 years, has amassed credentials and awards in virtually every aspect of media, including television, film and theater, as well as communications experience in corporate, commercial and non-profit settings. In July 2001, Rami joined his wife to expand her company to include Mixed Media Technology, a progressive multimedia design and consultant division. "From concept to completion, we design the most contemporary 'high-end' project that will accurately portray and communicate our clients' image and philosophy," says Rami. Diversity is the thing that truly distinguishes his work at Masequa Myers & Associates, he says. "I set out to create a tapestry of color representative of the mosaic of this country," he says. "I try to create projects that have meaning. The ideal situation is to find a project that has creative as well as educational components."

OFFICE OF THE GOVERNOR
207 State House
Springfield, Illinois 62706

JB PRITZKER
GOVERNOR

FILED
INDEX DEPARTMENT

APR 03 2020

IN THE OFFICE OF
SECRETARY OF STATE

April 3, 2020

The Honorable Jesse White
Secretary of State
Index Division
111 East Monroe
Springfield, IL 62706

Re: Appointment of Pemon Rami
       as a Member of the Illinois Arts Council

Dear Secretary White:

Effective immediately and upon filing of the Oath of Office with the Secretary of State, I have made the appointment of the following person as member, who shall execute the powers and discharge the duties vested in law in the office indicated.

NAME & ADDRESS	SALARY	EXP DATE	FORMER HOLDER
Pemon Rami	Expenses	4/3/2024	Tim Touhy

Sincerely,

Governor

When Blackness was Golden

17B ADENUBI CLOSE OFF TOYIN IKEJA LAGOS
www.ama-awards.com info@ama-awards.com 234 1 7397248

30th June, 2017.

PEMON RAMI

Dear Sir,

RE: AMAA 2017 NOMINATION NOTIFICATION FOR PEMON RAMI

We will like to congratulate PEMON RAMI for his nomination in AMAA 2017 Award for Best Nigerian Film for the movie "93 DAYS".

We herewith advise that with this letter we have invited the above named person to the 13th edition of the Africa Movie Academy Awards (AMAA) scheduled for Saturday, 15th July, 2017 at Eko Hotels and Suites, Victoria Island, Lagos.

AMAA is an offshoot of the Africa Film Academy – an initiative of the Osigwe Anyiam Osigwe Foundation, an organization geared towards research, training and propagating film making in Africa. Established in 2005, AMAA is conceptualized as an annual celebration of the brightest and the best in the African film industry. AMAA is the most prestigious and glamorous entertainment industry event of its kind in Africa.

The Board of AMAA and the Osigwe -Anyiam-Osigwe Foundation will be looking forward to seeing you at the event.

We thank you for your understanding and co-operation.

Yours faithfully,

Tony Anih
Director of Administration
Africa Movie Academy Awards

Touched by the greatest creation Black Women!

Val Gray Ward

Dr. Barbara Sizemore

Top row: Masequa and my sister Barbara
Bottom row: Masequa's Mom and My Mom

Dr. Dorothy Height

Marla Gibbs

Barbara Ann Teer

Dr. Carol Adams

Sarudzayi Sevanhu

Dr. Gwendolyn Baker

A few influential women in my life! What an honor to know them!
Pemon Rami

Those led by love always end up in the right place.

When Blackness was Golden

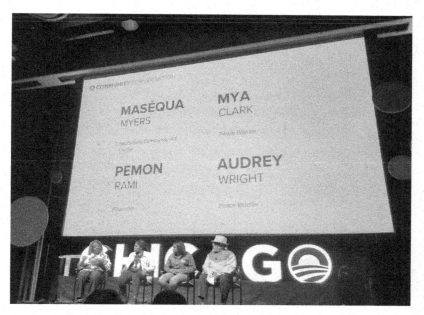

June 19, 2018, Maséqua and I were invited to participate as mainstage speakers for the Obama Foundation's Chicago Community Conversation entitled "Rooted in Chicago" held at the University of Illinois at Chicago.

THE HIST☉RYMAKERS.

PROUDLY ANNOUNCES THAT
THE VIDEO ORAL HISTORY INTERVIEW OF
PEMON RAMI
IS NOW A PERMANENT PART
OF THE HISTORYMAKERS COLLECTION AT
THE LIBRARY OF CONGRESS

"The HistoryMakers archive provides invaluable first-person accounts of both well-known and unsung African Americans, detailing their hopes, dreams and accomplishments—often in the face of adversity. This culturally important collection is a rich and diverse resource for scholars, teachers, students and documentarians seeking a more complete record of our nation's history and its people."

-James H. Billington, 13th Librarian of Congress
(June 1, 1929 – November 20, 2018)

Carla D. Hayden
14th Librarian of Congress

Julieanna L. Richardson
Founder & President, The HistoryMakers

THE HIST☉RYMAKERS.

PROUDLY ANNOUNCES THAT
THE VIDEO ORAL HISTORY INTERVIEW OF
MASÉQUA MYERS
IS NOW A PERMANENT PART
OF THE HISTORYMAKERS COLLECTION AT
THE LIBRARY OF CONGRESS

"The HistoryMakers archive provides invaluable first-person accounts of both well-known and unsung African Americans, detailing their hopes, dreams and accomplishments—often in the face of adversity. This culturally important collection is a rich and diverse resource for scholars, teachers, students and documentarians seeking a more complete record of our nation's history and its people."

-James H. Billington, 13th Librarian of Congress
(June 1, 1929 – November 20, 2018)

Carla D. Hayden
14th Librarian of Congress

Julieanna L. Richardson
Founder & President, The HistoryMakers

When Blackness was Golden

Appearance on *Windy City Live* with
Ryan Chiaverini, Val Warner,
and Rev. Otis Moss Jr. Photo credit:

Appearance on ABC News with
Judy Hsu and Terrell Brown

Hosting a talk show on WVON radio

STATE OF ILLINOIS

RICHARD H. NEWHOUSE
STATE SENATOR • 24TH DISTRICT
1900 E. 71ST STREET • CHICAGO, ILLINOIS 60649 • 312/643-4500

CAPITOL BUILDING • ROOM 121C • SPRINGFIELD, ILLINOIS 62706 • 217/782-5338

April 17, 1981

Suzanne K. Swanson
Coordinator
Artists-In-Residence Program
Illinois Arts Council
111 North Wabash Avenue
Chicago, Illinois

Dear Ms. Swanson:

   In my fourteen year tenure as Senator from the twenty-fourth district I have encountered few artists who combine artistic with administrative talent; professionalism with community concern; and, the energy to put such a combination to productive ends. Those assets describe Pemon Rami who has applied to the Council to become an artist in Residence in Chicago.

   As a member of the Arts Council of the National Association of State Legislators I have frquently used Pemon as an example of that rare artistic talent capable of drawing people easily into his art concepts.

   I highly recommend Pemon Rami to you and my office stands ready to cooperate with him and the Arts Council in a program we all wish to flourish.

Sincerely,

Richard H. Newhouse
State Senator

A letter of support from my favorite State Senator
Richard Newhouse

When Blackness was Golden

With Dick Gregory

This picture was taken on location when I was directing a documentary featuring Rev. Dr. Jeremiah A. Wright, Jr. and Rev. Jesse Jackson

With actor Anthony Mackie

With Diane Nash an American civil rights activist, leader and strategist of the student wing of the Student Nonviolent Coordinating Committee

With Richard Hunt one of the most important American sculptors of the 20th century. Richard holds the distinction as one of the foremost African-American abstract sculptors and artists.

When Blackness was Golden

At rehearsal for a play I directed in Los Angeles with Whitman Mayo Jr., an actor, best known for his role as Grady Wilson on the 1970s television sitcom *Sanford and Son*.

With Woodie King Jr., a director and producer of stage and screen, as well as the founding director of the New Federal Theatre in New York

Visiting with our friend Wayne Linsey; musician, producer, arranger, songwriter, artist and keyboardist for the Tonight Show.

Hanging with Regina Taylor, award-winning actress and playwright and Barbara Allen, Award-winning producer, director, and editor.

Producing an industrial film narrated by Angela Bassett

On location with (L to R) writer Sam Greenlee, Ron Pitts (first Black TV camera operator in Chicago and Robert Townsend. Seated, director of photography Joe Jody Williams, Back row director Carl Seaton.
Photo credit: Tacuma Rami

When Blackness was Golden

Seeing billboards in Africa advertising our film, *93 Days*, with my name on them was a wonderful feeling.

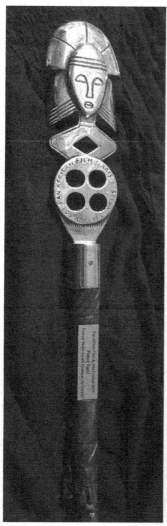

In 2017 I was awarded the Visionary Feature Film Award at the 25th Pan African Film Festival in Los Angeles

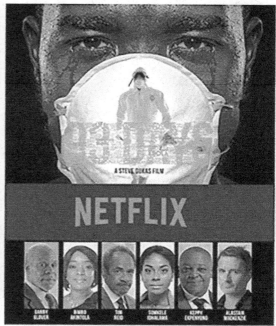

Speaking at the State of Illinois *Juneteenth Celebration*

Hanging out in Trinidad with LeRoy Clarke at his home. Leroy is considered one of Trinidad and Tobago's finest contemporary artists. LeRoy became an ancestor in July 2021

Spending time with Don Newcombe, the third black pitcher to appear in a major-league game. As a rookie he was selected to appear in the 1949 All-Star Game. Newcombe would go on to win the Rookie of the Year Award as well as becoming the first recipient of the Cy Young Award.

With Ayuko Babu founder of Pan African Film Festival and member of the board of jurors of Africa Movie Academy Awards.

When Blackness was Golden

Chuck D. from the rap group *Public Enemy*

Late comedian Paul Mooney attended the Los Angeles premiere for *Of Boys and Men.*

Moderating a discussion at the DuSable Museum of African American History with actor Delroy Lindo

Once the Zeno theatre construction was completed, staff went to high schools and door-to-door in the community to recruit. That's how we first encountered Walter King, the Spellbinder. In Walter, I saw the same things I'd seen in Paul Butler, L. Scott Caldwell, Robert Townsend, Maséqua Myers, and Doug Alan Mann when they worked with me early in their careers, a capacity for greatness and extreme talent. By the second year, I had raised $250,000 through grants and ticket sales and brought on full-time staff.

When Blackness was Golden

I created the Cultural Arts Program, which was designed to broaden the horizon of Black artists and artistry by application, education, and creation. The program was a medium through which the Black community could effectively express its culture.

The Cultural Arts program included:

- A 250-seat theatre
- Youth theatre development program
- Playwright's workshop
- Adult theatre classes
- African and jazz dance classes
- Series of special projects, including the publication of the Black Theatre Bulletin
- Music program — voice and basic piano
- Art program
- Performing arts theatre company

With Najwa planning a production

I recruited an incredible staff, including Ted Ward - director of the playwright's workshop, Barry Ray - theatre instructor, Jami Ayinde (Jerry Johnson) - music and piano instructor, Prince Nora - set design and lighting instructor, Arnell (Najwa) Pugh - dance instructor and choreographer, and Alicia Peterson - costume design.

Maséqua Myers was hired as assistant cultural arts director and Ajabu Children's Theatre director. She took on the task of founding and developing the Ajabu (which means wonderful and fantastic) Children's Theatre. The theatre earned the distinction of being Chicago's first professional children's theatre company featuring child actors and staff. It also meant she had to do everything: run day-to-day operations, coordinate training programs, write grants, form parent auxiliaries, develop scripts, supervise touring productions, direct, teach, and act — the works.

Arnell (Najwa) Pugh was our resident dance instructor and choreographer. Najwa had performed with icons like Duke Ellington, Count Basie, and Julian Swain. She studied African dance with Asadata Dafora, Baba Dinizulu, and Babatunde Olatunji and fire dance at the Cat and Fiddle Club in the Bahamas. I was able to surround myself with outstanding talent such as musicians Tony Llorens, Chico

When Blackness was Golden

Freeman, Amina Myers, and Harold (Atu) Murray. Harold Ray was our graphics designer and art instructor, and John Clay, our master technician.

Maséqua and I were both in deep. For more than five years, we were seriously committed, creatively recognized, rewarded, and awarded. While at BBF, I also became a founding board member of the Chicago and Midwest Black Theatre alliances and a founding board member of the League of Chicago Theatres. Maséqua was presented the "Best Actress Award" in Chicago's One-Act Play Festival, and my production of Runako Jahi's first produced play, *Mainline Blues*, won first place.

At the same time, Maséqua enrolled in Northeastern Illinois University's University Without Walls–Theatre Management and Production program.

Amidst our work, we married on the set of an African village built for Maséqua's production of *The Strong Breed*, written by Wole Soyinka, the Pulitzer Prize award-winning Nigerian playwright.

On Sunday, May 4, 1975, our African wedding was held. The wedding was officiated by Dr. Anderson Thompson in English and Elkin M. Sithole, a South African senior professor of ethnomusicology and anthropology at Northeastern Illinois University, in the South African language, Zulu. Over two hundred people attended our wedding.

Dr. Anderson Thompson and Elkin M. Sithole, officiating our wedding

Following the wedding, we spent the beginning of our honeymoon visiting my grandmother Savannah in Haskell, Oklahoma, on her eighty-acre farm.

We had a layover in Atlanta. On the plane, we saw an advertisement for a downtown hotel that had a swimming pool in its suite. We decided to get one of those rooms and stay in Atlanta for a few days. After Atlanta, we flew to Oklahoma and then to Los Angeles, which was fantastic.

And as if running a theatre and having a new wife was not enough, when we returned to Chicago Abena Joan Brown, one of the founders of ETA Creative Arts Foundation, called to ask me if I was available to provide transportation for blind jazz multi-instrumentalist Rahsaan Roland Kirk at his hotel and after his shows at the Jazz Showcase.

Rahsaan played tenor saxophone, flute, and as many as four wind instruments at the same time. Watching Rahsaan perform with his band and feeling his music was nothing less than an experience of greatness! Rahsaan and I became friends, and I would drive him around whenever he was in Chicago.

Rahsaan Roland Kirk having breakfast at my apartment following his show at the Jazz Showcase

Chicago Black Theatre Community

The Black theatre community had a resurgence during the late '60s and early '70s. Numerous groups began sprouting up to provide creative experiences for their audiences.

Black Theatres and Companies in Chicago: 1960s–1980s

- Affro Arts Theatre — Phil Cochran and the Artistic Heritage Ensemble
- Ajabu Children's Theatre — Maséqua Myers
- Black Heritage Theatrical Players — Rev. Spencer Jackson Family
- Chicago Black Ensemble — Jackie Taylor
- Chicago Theatre Company — Douglas Alan Mann, Michael Perkins, Chuck Smith, and Charles Finister

- Cultural Messengers — H. Mark Williams
- ETA Creative Arts Foundation — Okoro Harold Johnson and Abena Joan Brown
- Independent Professional Performing Artists — Pemon Rami and Maséqua Myers
- Ira Rodgers — Writer/Producer/Director
- Jerry Jones — Producer/Director
- Kusema Players — Van Jackson
- Kuumba Workshop — Val Gray Ward and Francis Ward
- LaMont Zeno Theatre — Pemon Rami, Maséqua Myers, and Useni Perkins
- New Concept Theatre — Lawrence Kabaka and Marcus Nelson
- New Era Theatre — Rodney Graham
- Newer Still Theatre — John Houston
- Oscar Brown Jr. Productions
- South Side Center for the Performing Arts — Ted Ward and Pemon Rami
- X-BAG Experimental Black Actors Guild — Clarence Taylor, Claudia McCormick, and Jean Davidson

When Blackness was Golden

In 1974, companies united to form the Chicago Black Theatre Alliance to promote and foster better relationships between Black theatre groups. Original members included Van Jackson (Kusema), Rev. Spencer Jackson (Black Heritage Theatrical Players), Okoro Harold Johnson (ETA), Marcus Nelson (New Concept), Useni Perkins (BBF), Pemon Rami (Zeno), Clarence Taylor (X-BAG), and Val Gray Ward (Kuumba). Our aim was to become more relevant and accountable to the Black community as well as improving the quality of the Black theatre in Chicago.

In 1976, I was invited to New York to meet with Duane Jones, then executive director of the National Black Theatre Alliance, Hazel Bryant, and a few of their board members to discuss the Chicago Black Theatre Alliance joining their federation of African-American theatre companies in New York. It was my position following the meeting that there was no true benefit to the Chicago Alliance joining. The Chicago Black Theatre Alliance would not have a voice nor influence in the primarily New York organization and, as such, I felt we should continue our separate but supportive paths. When I returned to Chicago and met with the members of our alliance, we declined their offer. Additionally, we reached out to surrounding states to form the Midwest Black Theatre Alliance.

During everything we were involved in, on November 29, 1976, our second son, Tacuma Akintunde (alert: second son), was born.

Diversity, like integration, did not serve the interest of Chicago's Black theatre community!

As demonstrated by the number of companies listed above, the Black theatre community was growing exponentially during the '70s while defining Black aesthetics and generating new audiences. Diversity was defined as "the practice or quality of including or involving people from a range of different social and ethnic backgrounds."

During the '70s, the African-American theatre community was struggling to find its identity, audience, and funding to grow the individual and collective movement. When the dominant cultural group began to focus on increasing diversity, it was prompted by a call from the Black community to stop the exclusion of Black creatives from the general Chicago theatre movement.

The socio-political issue of funding the arts shifted to define diversity as White theatres having access to more Black audiences and not the other way around. Larger institutions banded together to create their own version of diversifying. The established "White" theatres that had traditionally ignored or limited the involvement of Black actors and audiences at their institutions started targeting our audiences in attempts to secure available funding from the diversity pot! This move, in most cases, blocked Black theatres from receiving funding support while encouraging Theatres like the Goodman, Steppenwolf, and Victory Gardens to produce their "one Black play" per season. There was no consideration for funding Black theatres to diversify their audiences by recruiting other cultural groups to attend our performances — only the reverse. As with the Negro Baseball League, once a Black play was produced at a major downtown or northside theatre, Black audiences flocked there, leaving most of their own community theatres to wither away.

When Blackness was Golden

London, England, and the Royal Shakespearian Festival

In 1975, I was invited (as director of the LaMont Zeno Theatre) to attend a residency with the Royal Shakespeare Company, a major British theatre company based in Stratford-upon-Avon, Warwickshire, England, where William Shakespeare was born and raised. I shared the invitation and exciting news with Useni Eugene Perkins, then director of BBF, who agreed to my attending and stated BBF would cover the cost. At that same time, we were touring the production of *The Black Fairy* and were scheduled to open the show in Detroit, Michigan. When I was informed Detroit Mayor Coleman Young was going to present the Key to the City and a proclamation from the city council to us, I declined the invitation to London.

The production in Detroit was outstanding. All shows sold out. As my reputation grew nationwide, tension between Perkins and me increased. I had just turned twenty-five and was assertive, self-confident, militant, and talented. I never saw myself as a follower. I could separate my relationship in public from my work relationship at BBF, but Perkins couldn't. He saw himself as my boss in the building or on a national stage and tried to control me, which was impossible!

So, a few years later in 1978, when I was again invited to the Royal Shakespearian Festival, I approached Perkins about attending. He said I couldn't go. No justification. Just no. I replied he couldn't tell me I couldn't go; he could only say that BBF wouldn't pay for it. Maséqua and I used vacation days and paid for the trip ourselves. This was the beginning of the end of our relationship with Perkins, BBF, and the LaMont Zeno Theatre.

The British Airways flight to London was eight hours, and it was my first trip out of the country. Exciting! The festival that year was held in January, and London was biting cold.

The city was drab, and their monuments reminded me too much of slavery. But we participated in workshops and saw over twenty productions.

Between theatres, we visited most of the famous sites: Buckingham Palace, Big Ben, the Houses of Parliament, Downing Street, The London Dungeon, Tower Bridge, The Tower of London, Hyde Park Speakers' Corner, Madame Tussauds, Regent's Park, Piccadilly Circus, The National Gallery, Downing Street, Stonehenge, Trafalgar Square, and Westminster Abbey. Shakespeare's house at Stratford-upon-Avon was another of the places we visited.

We toured the Royal British Museum, which was housed in a former mental institution building. A large pit out front was at least seven feet deep. The tour guide explained they used to put "crazy people" in the pit and rent poles for visitors to beat the crazy out of them! They really believed that was a way to cure mental illness back then.

Maséqua and I stayed in the Eltham community in southeast London, England, within the Royal Borough of Greenwich. We lived with a kind, young bobby (policeman) and his wife for the first week we were in London to get the lay of the land, and then we moved into hotels. It was cold! I could never get warm enough! I even bought a full-length lamb skin coat, which didn't help much. It hurt when I realized how much I paid for it with the exchange rate!

The theatre experience was incredible! We saw Agatha Christie's *The Mousetrap*, a murder mystery play which opened in the West End of London in 1952 and had been running continuously in the same theatre. *A Chorus Line* and numerous Shakespeare plays filled our evenings and weekends. Our nights were spent in the pubs.

Back to the U.S. and Chicago

By 1979, I was overworked, producing a seven-production season at Zeno, casting feature films, writing a column for Night Moves newspaper, directing plays, and teaching acting. When I missed a grant deadline for the National Endowment for the Arts, Donald Blackwell, an actor who worked with us and a supervisor for the Chicago Postal Service, told me he could take care of having the postage backdated. He would make sure it was mailed, and I agreed.

I'm not sure how, but when Perkins found out, he went to the board of directors to insist they allow him to fire me. My national reputation had outgrown the tiny hole Perkins attempted to place me in, and I felt my growth intimidated him. He also worked to fire Maséqua and dismantled my staff. The theatre program was never the same.

When Perkins attempted to block Maséqua from receiving unemployment benefits, she took him to arbitration and won.

When I was fired from BBF, my skills as a director and casting director grew in demand. Val Gray Ward invited me to direct several productions at her Kuumba Theatre, including *The Sirens, Mighty Gents, Jolly Green Soldier,* and *Mzilikazi.* I also directed *Livin Fat* at the Black Arts Celebration. I produced touring productions for Chicago Public Libraries titled, *Go Tell It On The Mountain* and *Christmas Past and Present,* which were featured on Bozo's Circus (WGN).

I was recruited as a talent agent by Althea Knowles to join her at AB Modeling and Talent Agency, where I provided talent for the television, film, print, and theatre productions, including The Goodman *Theatre Death and The Kings Horseman* and *Native Son.*

I became a consultant to the newly formed Illinois film office, working with Lucy Salenger. Ironically, I was hired as a consultant and evaluator for the National Endowment for the Arts (NEA), the organization for which I missed the proposal deadline. In that role, I traveled the country to arts organizations, evaluating whether they should receive NEA funding. Soon after, Maséqua and I established our own company, Mixed Media Productions. We continued producing and directing independent theatrical, video, multi-image, and film projects. Nudging, cajoling, coaxing, and encouraging each other, Maséqua and I were caught in an upwardly spiraling whirlwind. Acting here, producing/directing there, winning awards everywhere — we were skid marks on the road.

From Chicago's Goodman Theatre to The John F. Kennedy Center for the Performing Arts in Washington, D.C., Maséqua, as an actress, was in demand throughout the U.S. and abroad. Capturing a lead role in the U.S. premiere of Wole Soyinka's *Death and the King's Horseman* garnered her coverage in local and national newspapers and magazines.

Additionally, for her stellar work, she was presented with the Chicago Black Theatre Alliance Award for Best Lead Actress. She was nominated for a Joseph Jefferson Award for her incredible performance in the Victory Gardens production of *Eden* by Steve Carter and directed by Chuck Smith. We literally went around the country producing plays, including *Guys and Dolls*, *The Wiz*, and *Bubbling Brown Sugar* at the Kalamazoo Civic Theatre.

We continued working on films as well, including *Blues Brothers*, *Welcome to Success*, *One in A Million*, and *Dummy*. In our "leisure time," we produced thirty-three talk radio shows under the theme *"A Taste of Culture"* on WBMX radio, reaching more than 300,000 listeners weekly.

When Blackness was Golden

In addition, I continued my weekly entertainment column in the *Night Moves* newspaper.

I directed our second production of Maséqua's one-woman show, *Quiet Before the Storm*, produced by Jackie Taylor for the Chicago Black Ensemble at Victory Gardens Theatre. The show received raving reviews, primarily because of Maséqua's superb acting but also because of the show's technical design by me and John Clay. I was incorporating multimedia techniques way before "multimedia" was even an established word!

The critics began to recognize what I discovered years before — Maséqua was talented beyond measure.

Maséqua performed multiple characters during her one-woman show!

A few of the show's reviews:

".... She is embracingly talented, capable of flights that last long and go deep." Chicago Sun Times

".... with effortless ease, Miss Myers demonstrates that she belongs in the company of the great female actresses we have known in this century! Earl Calloway - Chicago Defender

".... She's heavy! It's good to see I'm not fighting the battle alone." Esther Rolle (Good Times)

".... Myers' formidable arsenal of talent is thrown into all-out war on her material. This is impressive. "Richard Christianson - Chicago Tribune

Chapter Nine: Oscar Brown Jr.

"Education can be a tool of oppression or freedom."
                              Pemon Rami

The late Oscar Brown Jr. was my mentor, creative inspiration, and friend. I can only imagine where I would be if I had not seen his production of *Lyrics of Sunshine and Shadow*.

I was glued to the television when the Smothers Brothers' CBS television show featured Oscar's song, *"Opportunity Please Knock."* The show's cast comprised members of the Chicago youth gang known as the Blackstone Rangers.

I was also in the audience soaking up Oscar's style as he and Jean Pace joined with Brazilian musicians Luiz Henrique and Sivuca in the production of *Joy 69* which "ran" in Chicago. I had the great fortune of being an Oscar magnet. Whenever I would travel, I would run into Oscar or he would be performing in various cities I was visiting, such as Atlanta, Washington, DC, and New York.

When Malcolm X College opened its doors in 1970, Oscar and I were among the Chicago's Black talent elite hired as artists-in-residence. Oscar produced and directed his musical *Slave Story*, the first play presented in the new state-of-the-art theatre. I produced and directed the second production, titled *M(ego) and the Green Ball of Freedom*, written by Ron Milner.

Slave Story was written in iambic pentameter (five double beats, or ten syllables, with emphasis placed on every second beat) and rhymed quatrains which is a grouping of four lines.

In 1973, Oscar permitted me to produce and direct *Slave Story* at the Lamont Zeno Theatre on the West Side of

Chicago. Oscar was proudly in the audience supporting my effort.

In 1978, I produced and directed the first iteration of *Quiet Before the Storm,* Maséqua's One Woman Show, at the LaMont Zeno Theatre, which featured Oscar Brown's songs. In 1981, I reimagined the show as a cabaret version, which I produced at artist Douglas Williams' Brief Reflections Night Club in Chicago, with Oscar Brown Jr. in attendance.

Maséqua, Elroy Young, and Oscar Brown Jr. at the Brief Reflections Night Club in Chicago following Maséqua performance of *Quiet before the Storm.*

When Blackness was Golden

In Los Angeles, I modified the show again and renamed it *Thru the Eyes of Women*, which also utilized several original Oscar Brown Jr. songs and was produced in 1995 at the Complex Theatre in Hollywood.

When I relocated to Phoenix, Arizona, to manage the Black Theatre Troupe in April 1982, I called on Oscar Brown Jr. once again to lend his support. Oscar did more; he granted permission for me to create a new musical titled *Fresh*, based upon his songs. *Fresh* had a very successful run. The production toured the State of Arizona, and Oscar proudly attended opening night!

When I moved to Los Angeles in January 1989, Oscar was a frequent visitor to my home, and my family would attend his shows whenever he performed at the Jazz Bakery or any venue in L.A. One of Oscar's creative concepts he shared with me was D.O.M.E., a dramatic organization of musical expression. His concept was to take music, songs, and characters to create a story — a play without a script. Oscar saw a D.O.M.E. as a vehicle to organize and arrange various poems and compositions, and he created characters to produce a complete theatrical piece. I embraced Oscar's concept and used it to design various productions throughout my theatrical career.

Oscar Brown Jr. gave to the world treasures of music, poems, prose, and plays. "Music is nothing more than an organization of sounds and silence in relationships to time," he said. OBJ was awesome! He wrote and published 125-plus songs, and many became classics. This musical genius grew up in Bronzeville, Chicago, and his complex life greatly impacted mine.

It was 2003—the last time Oscar and I spent quality time together was at our home in Los Angeles. Oscar requested I produce and direct his play, *A Journey Through Forever*.

I was busy working on several projects, so I couldn't move forward on his request.

I was fortunate to visit Oscar in the hospital the day before he departed this life on May 29, 2005, in Chicago. He couldn't speak, but our eyes and spirits communicated.

From the collection of the Brown Family

Chapter Ten: Breaking into Feature Films

> "The only way to keep Black people from succeeding is to not let them compete!"
>
> Pemon Rami

When asked about my work on the TV shows and feature films such as *Bird of the Iron Feather* (1969), *The Spook Who Sat by the Door* (1973), *Cooley High* (1975) *Mahogany* (1975), *The Blues Brothers* (1980), *Of Boys and Men* (2008), or *93 Days* (2015), I remind myself and others that my pilgrimage to film production and theatre directing began early. It included many classes, personal studies, meetings, and conversations with elders that educated me to understand racial, social, and economic justice.

The Spook Who Sat by the Door

By 1972, my reputation as an actor, director, and producer was well-established in Chicago. I received a telephone call from Sam Greenlee, the renowned author of the best-selling book, *The Spook Who Sat by the Door*. Sam was in pre-production to shoot the film version of the book, which was to be directed by the legendary Ivan Dixon. Ivan was best known for his role as POW Staff Sergeant James Kinchloe in the hit TV series *Hogan's Heroes*. In 1964, he starred in the independent film, *Nothing but a Man*, and the cult classic, *Car Wash*.

Shortly after we shot Spook, I worked with Ivan as the Chicago casting director on the pilot for the television version of the feature film, *Cooley High*. The studio rejected the pilot, saying it wasn't funny enough, and opted to create the sitcom, *What's Happening,* starring Ernest Thomas who had been cast to play Preacher in the TV pilot. Glynn Turman famously played Preacher in the feature film.

Sam and Ivan requested I play Shorty Duncan, one of the pivotal characters in the film. Shorty was the drug dealer and numbers runner whose murder by the police leads to riots and the beginning of the insurrection. I readily agreed and was also hired to help cast the film.

Paul Butler, one of the actors I introduced to Sam, was cast to play Do Daddy Dean, a lead actor. I shot a few scenes in Chicago and Gary, but when the time came to shoot my speaking parts, the film ran out of money and was moved to L.A. I was also responsible for casting the extras for the film when we shot in Gary, Indiana. My first day of filming was on Sixty-Third and Cottage Grove walking down the street. My second day was shot in Gary, Indiana. Gary's first Black mayor, Richard Hatcher, gave the production major assistance with the film, including providing four abandoned city blocks to burn down during the riot scene.

I hired more than three hundred people for the riot scene, and all their checks bounced! By the time Sam and Ivan secured the money to pay the extras, they were angry because their first checks had bounced. We decided it was best to have all extras go to the police station in Gary to get paid.

A few weeks later, I received another call from Sam requesting that I fly to Hollywood to shoot my speaking scenes. I was on my way to the Land of LA LA! When I arrived at the airport in L.A., I was informed that one of the lead actors had been arrested for marijuana possession, so they had to stop by the jail and bail him out. The next day I was on location filming. There is nothing like the feeling you get making a movie on the streets of L.A. The crowds, requests for autographs, the star treatment, and the women—I had arrived! Sam and Ivan thought Lawrence

When Blackness was Golden

Cook and I should improvise our scene since we were theatre people. Ivan's sister, Audrey Stevenson, played my mother, Mrs. Duncan, in the film; however, we never met.

The film was based on Sam's best-selling novel of the same name. It was also the first movie scored by the great Herbie Hancock. Spook is the story of the first Black CIA agent who was hired to "show" the world the CIA had integrated and improved the chances of a U.S. senator to be reelected. He literally sat by the door for all the visitors to see. Maséqua was hired to play one of the main characters, Pretty Willie's girlfriend, even though her scenes were left on the cutting room floor. Maséqua provided her own wardrobe, but when filming was over, her clothes were taken to Los Angeles, and she never got them back.

When I arrived at the hotel in L.A., the cast members who played the Cobras gang in the film were trying to determine who knew how to cook greens. That job was left to me as the new arrival. When the movie opened in Chicago in 1973, it was quickly shut down by the FBI after a few days and the prints disappeared. Most of the cast members never worked in Hollywood again because of their participation in Spook. For years, the only way to obtain a copy of the film was the bootleg video Sam himself sold. He would say, "The movie is free, but my signature is twenty dollars."

In 2004, producer and director Tim Reid and his wife, Daphne Maxwell Reid, tracked down a negative of the film stored in a vault under a different name by Ivan Dixon. Tim and Daphne released the digitally remastered version on DVD.

Director Ivan Dixon asked me to slow down because the police couldn't catch me when I was filming this scene in the *Spook* playing "Shorty Duncan"

In 2012, with the assistance of Jacqueline Stewart, professor of cinema studies at the University of Chicago, *The Spook Who Sat by the Door* was named to the National Film Registry of the Library of Congress as one of the country's "culturally, historically, and aesthetically significant films." Following its selection, I had the great honor of hosting a screening of the film with Sam in attendance at the DuSable Museum of

African American History on February 17, 2013. Sam passed away May 19, 2014.

At Sam's request, I planned his memorial service for June 6, 2014, at the DuSable.

Three Tough Guys

When I returned to Chicago from filming Spook in Los Angeles, I received a phone call from Chicago's legendary talent agent Shirley Hamilton requesting that I play an extra in the movie *Three Tough Guys,* starring Lino Ventura, Isaac Hayes, and Fred Williamson. At first, I declined. I had just returned from California where I had a featured role in The Spook Who Sat by the Door, so I was not interested in being an extra. Shirley pleaded with me, so I reluctantly agreed. The scene I filmed as a background extra was on the street while Isaac Hayes walked by. Isaac kept looking at me when he walked by. Eventually, he stopped and asked me if we knew each other. After talking for a while between takes, he realized he recognized me from *The Spook Who Sat by the Door* screening he had seen. We spent quality time talking between takes and discovered we were both Leos! It was great spending time with the Oscar winner, even though his acting left a lot to be desired. A month or so after my encounter with Isaac Hayes, I received a call from Motown Productions requesting I provide casting services for the feature film, *Mahogany,* starring Diana Ross and Billy Dee Williams. Isaac had recommended me!

Mahogany

Mahogany was filmed in 1974 in Chicago and Rome. It was a romantic drama film directed originally by British filmmaker Tony Richardson. The film was produced by Motown Productions. Motown's founder Berry Gordy took over the film direction after firing Tony Richardson for creative differences.

Following the success of *Lady Sings the Blues*, *Mahogany* served as Ross' follow-up feature film. I was cast as one of Billy Dee Williams' campaign workers, along with Lenard Norris, Jerome Arnold, and Obelo Herscholt Polk.

Working on *Mahogany* for six weeks and watching the acting of Billy Dee Williams, Diana Ross, and Tony Perkins as well as the directing of Berry Gordy was invaluable to my development.

Me and Berry Gordy during filming of *Mahogany*

My work on *Mahogany* led to my being hired on fourteen feature films and television movies, including *Cooley High*, starring Glynn Turman and Lawrence Hilton Jacobs; *Uptown Saturday Night*, starring Sidney Poitier, Bill Cosby, Redd Foxx, and Richard Pryor; *Dummy*, starring Levar Burton; *One in a Million*, starring Levar Burton, Bea Richards, and Morgan Freeman; *Monkey Hustle*, starring

When Blackness was Golden

Yaphet Kotto and Rudy Ray Moore; *Torn Between Two Lovers,* starring Lee Remick and George Peppard; *Welcome to*

Success, starring Cicely Tyson and Morgan Freeman; and *The Blues Brothers.*

The Blues Brothers

Working on *The Blues Brothers* film was both a great experience and disappointing. The opportunity to meet and work with Cab Calloway, Aretha Franklin, James Brown, Ray Charles, John Belushi, and Dan Aykroyd was incredible! I was hired to coordinate the Chicago casting for extras and small speaking roles. During filming, over 10,000 people were employed. On the other hand, working with the film's director John Landis was a challenge and, at times, disappointing. When actor Vick Morrow and two children were killed during the filming of *Twilight Zone:* The Movie, which Landis also directed, I was not surprised! When we were filming *The Blues Brothers,* several extras were injured due to recklessness.

Several extras were asked to perform actions that should have been done by professional stunt men and women. Jumping off trucks and driving cars during the filming of chase scenes on Chicago's Lower Wacker Drive are minor examples. One of the local actors I hired crashed the squad car he was driving during one of the high-speed chase scenes on Lower Wacker Drive.

The day we shot the Maxwell Street scene outside of the restaurant that Aretha Franklin's character owned in the movie, I hired three hundred extras, including the dancers and the Johnny Lee Hooker Band that was playing on the street. If you watch closely, the harmonica player is there one minute and then gone! The filming took too long for him.

He'd started drinking early that day, so he was good and drunk when he decided he had enough and stumbled off!

The following day we shot the scene where Jake and Elwood drive the Bluesmobile across a bridge, making the marching Illinois Nazis jump in the water. The call sheet for that day required twenty-five cars with non-descript drivers. This means the cars will be the focus of the shot and not the people. I hired extras from the Maxwell Street scene who just happened to be Black but owned the type of cars required.

On the day of filming, John Landis asked me why it was so dark out there. He was asking why there were so many Black people on set. I explained to him my thinking since the call sheet only called for cars. Landis replied, "I wanted my set to be seventy percent white and thirty percent Black like the way of the world." "What world are you referring to?" I asked. "Landis responded that it was the way he wanted it on his film set."

Everyone who had a production office was required to keep in stock a six pack of Dr. Pepper in case Landis stopped by for a meeting. When he did come to my casting office, he would drink his Dr. Pepper and belch! Disgusting! Aside from Landis, *The Blues Brothers* experience was incredible but tense.

Original *Blues Brothers* crew button

When Blackness was Golden

My mentors: Oscar Brown Jr., Sam Greenlee, and Okoro Harold Johnson

In 1975, I began working as a location scout with Lucy Salenger, the new director of the Illinois Film Office. In many ways, Lucy was responsible for rebuilding the on-location film business in Illinois. I was one of the consultants they would contact when film companies were scouting for a city and state for their project in which to film. I would escort the production team around the city. Most of the time, I ended up providing casting or location services for the films or TV shows.

One in a Million: The Ron LeFlore Story

In 1977, William Clarkson, the unit production manager on the film *Mahogany*, hired me to provide casting and location services for the made-for-TV biographical sports drama,

One in a Million: The Ron LeFlore Story. The TV movie starred twenty-year-old LeVar Burton in his first film role following his highly successful appearance as Kunta Kinte in *Roots*.

Dolores Robinson (Holly Robinson Peete's mother) was LeVar's manager at the time and was incredible to work with. Her thirteen-year-old daughter Holly was often on the set learning the ropes; to watch Dolores teaching Holly was a lesson in patience and motivation.

One in a Million told the story of Ron LeFlore, a troubled Detroit youth, from his heroin addiction to his time in Jackson State Penitentiary, and his discovery in prison by Billy Martin, who was then the manager of the Detroit Tigers.

The TV movie was filmed at Statesville prison. Walking in and hearing the slamming of the prison doors was unsettling. I was responsible for casting inmates for roles at the prison. As the guards marched the inmates into the cell where I was holding the auditions I was scared knowing I had to tell criminals they couldn't play criminals in a movie. It turned out several of the inmates knew me from Stateway Gardens.

One of my proud moments while working on this film was having James Hyman a.k.a. "Bubbles," who was a member of our little league baseball team, become a member of the cast. "James" was a great ballplayer and could have played in the major leagues if not for life circumstances.

"Bubbles" worked as LeVar's baseball double during the filming in Statesville prison. I made a priority of reaching back to talented people I had met over the years to give them an opportunity to be in a movie. Our eldest son Babatunde, who was seven at the time, was featured at the end of the film in a speaking role with LeVar.

When Blackness was Golden

The TV movie first aired on CBS on September 26, 1978, and was released theatrically in Europe.

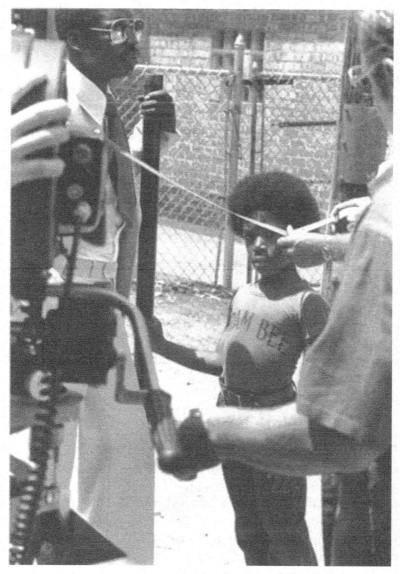

Our (then) seven-year-old son Babatunde featured in the film with LeVar

Dummy

Approximately a year later, I was hired by casting director Lisa Clarkson (Bill's sister) to provide casting and location services for the TV movie *Dummy*, which also starred LeVar Burton. The movie was based on Ernest Tidyman's nonfiction book of the same name. The film also starred Paul Sorvino, Brian Dennehy, Helen Martin, Holly Robinson (Peete), and Chicago actors Paul Butler, Frankie Hill, Tricia Borha, Obilo, Ira Rogers, Irma Riley, James Spinks, Nathan Davis, Yaumilton Brown, Lorenzo Clemons, and Steven Williams.

Dummy is the story of Donald Lang, a young African American who was born deaf. Donald is arrested and charged with the murder of a prostitute he was seen leaving a bar with, then convicted and sent to a mental institution. A role in the script was described as a Black giant. The first person I thought of was Ray Price, a former football player who grew up with me in Stateway Gardens. Ray Price was cast in the film. I also hired most of the extras for the prison scenes from people I knew from Stateway Gardens projects. The film was shot in the Cook County Jail. Despite multiple warnings about not taking in contraband, one of the crew was arrested for having cocaine in his pocket on the first day of filming. *Dummy* aired first in the USA in May 1979, then in the Netherlands, Italy, and Germany.

Even though I ended up working on some films that became classics, I was also offered many opportunities I couldn't accept because of the negative portrayal of Black people. As a matter of fact, I was told I was developing a bad reputation in Hollywood. While I was scouting locations for a film, we visited a home in an affluent Chicago neighborhood on the north side. The owners were offered $1,000 per day to allow us the use of their home and grant us permission to redecorate their home in whatever fashion was necessary.

When Blackness was Golden

They also would compensate them for the phone and electricity bills, if used. Some families were offered the option to stay in a hotel during filming.

When we arrived at the Black family's home, the owner was only offered $500 per day and none of the other reimbursements as the other north side homeowner. A few days before the filming began, I called the family and suggested they call the film office and tell them they changed their minds. The film company made them a much better offer which included many of the same things they offered the north side family. The company assumed I told them what was going on. They couldn't prove it was me, but it became a mark against me. Oh well! This is an example of the type of issues I faced.

Another example would be during the winter on the days we would have non-Black extras. There would be buses for people to keep warm inside. On days that most of the extras were Black, there would be no such accommodations. Further, when I arrived on location, I could tell the type of people who were working that day by the type of food being served.

By the time I had completed *The Blues Brothers*, I was all over the place! I had a radio show on WBMX entitled *A Taste of Culture* and an entertainment column in Night Moves weekly newspaper. I was directing plays, producing music, and still working on films. I was exhausted. My eye and throat were infected, and I was having colon spasms. My doctor told me it was all related to stress, and if I didn't change my lifestyle, it would get worse. So, I decided I would make my services available to other theatres around the country. I admit it was a cavalier idea, but it worked. I got job offers, but it only minimized the stress.

Blaxploitation Films

I have always been bothered by the term "blaxploitation" films, which is often used to describe African-American themed films made in the 1970s. When Melvin Van Peebles wrote, directed, and starred in *Sweet Sweetback's Baadasssss Song*, it was a groundbreaking film that spearheaded the rush of African-American action films. Van Peebles' work proved it was possible to make movies created for Black audiences by Black filmmakers and financed by Black people. It also opened the door for the development of what became known as blaxploitation.

As a member of the film community during that period who worked on over fourteen feature films, I am offended by use of that term. Blaxploitation films should be defined as films produced by white run studios, featuring African-American actors in lead roles, usually with anti-establishment plots but minimal African-American participation behind the scenes in production development, writing, directing, or producing roles.

These films were created primarily to take advantage of the emerging new Black audience hungry to see films that had Black people cast in lead roles. The fact that Van Peeples used mostly his own money and relied largely on Black actors and technicians means it does not fit into the blaxploitation category.

Sweetback told the story of one Black man's battle against white authority. The film scored a huge success with African-American audiences. I contend that films like *Blacula,* Fred Williamson's many films, *Thomasine & Bushrod* (directed by Gordon Parks Jr.)., *Melinda* (written by Lonne Elder III), *Shaft in Africa, Mahogany, Cooley High, Uptown Saturday Night,* and *The Spook Who Sat by the Door* should not be included in the canon of blaxploitation films.

Chapter Eleven: Directing on the Road

When actors ask me over the years if they should relocate to Los Angeles or New York, I always say they should first master their market. Maséqua and I mastered the Chicago market. We had received national recognition for our work, and I began to receive invitations from theatres around the country.

In 1981, Jim Carver, then-director of the Kalamazoo Civic Theatre in Kalamazoo, Michigan, called about my directing their production of *The Wiz*. When Jim Carver called, I was reluctant to go. I'm not sure why. Maséqua suggested I call Jim back because it sounded to her like I came off as uninterested and she was right. When I phoned him back, I got the impression he felt the same as she did, but I convinced him I was interested, and he offered me the job.

The Kalamazoo Civic is a beautiful 600-seat facility in downtown Kalamazoo, Michigan, located across from city hall. Our production of *The Wiz* included a cast of fifty actors, singers, and dancers, a twenty-four-piece orchestra, and opened to rave reviews. While in Kalamazoo, Michigan, the Black Theatre Troupe in Phoenix, Arizona, called the Civic Theatre in search of a director for their upcoming production of *Runaways*, a musical written by Elizabeth Swados, about the lives of children who run away from home and are homeless.

The late Helen Mason, founder of the Black Theatre Troupe, convinced me to travel to Phoenix and direct their production, when she explained it was seventy-five degrees.

Production of *The Wiz* I directed at the Kalamazoo Civic Theatre in 1981, featuring Jamila Ajibade as Dorothy, Chan Pratt as the Scarecrow, Myron Simon as the Tin Man, and Cliff Brown as the Lion

It just so happened that year was one of the coldest years on record in the Midwest, and it was ten below zero in Michigan when I got the call. Even though I didn't particularly like the play, and I had also received a request from the Mule Barn Theatre in Tarkio, Missouri Phoenix was where I decided to go for the weather. Helen was impressed with my work and asked me to stay on for the remainder of their season as the artistic director. I took the job, going with the flow. Although Maséqua and I had reservations about taking our young sons to lily-White Phoenix, it presented opportunities we couldn't ignore. And, having been involved in integrating her grade school as a pre-teen, Maséqua was prepared to keep our children grounded. We had no idea how racially negative the experience would be for them.

Moving our sons to a White community in a Republican state was not a good idea. The racism was palpable!

When Blackness was Golden

Our family was confronted by discrimination and racism on every front.

We felt that because we had a key presence within the Black community in Phoenix, that would be a saving grace. It was not!

We relocated from Chicago and the South Side, specifically, which was a safe haven for us and our children. I apologized for putting them in that position and still regret it to this day. They survived it but at a cost.

While I was there as artistic director, the theatre troupe's audience grew in numbers, budget, and in recognition. Things ran smoothly at the theatre the first year. The second year, I was invited back to Kalamazoo to direct their production of *Guys and Dolls*. I agreed. *Guys and Dolls* is a musical with lyrics and music by Frank Loesser and book by Jo Swerling and Abe Burrows. The show premiered on Broadway in 1950 and won a Tony Award for Best Musical. The Civic opted to do a version of the play with a Black cast and director. The production was well-received. I stuck to the original script for the most part, however, I added two songs by Earth, Wind & Fire.

In the meantime, Maséqua was contracted to direct the Black Theatre Troupe's production of *Bubbling Brown Sugar* while I was away. Bubbling tells the story of Harlem in its golden years. Taking many of the great songs from the era, Loften Mitchell wrote the story of a bygone era. This musical started a whole wave of Broadway shows by and about Black composers. It had a lengthy Broadway run and both national and European tours.

My Kalamazoo production of *Guys and Dolls* went flawlessly, and I returned to Phoenix a few days before the opening of Bubbling. Then the worst thing happened.

Return to Phoenix

During Maséqua's dress rehearsal, I went to buy a gallon of paint to have the room painted where we were going to hold the opening night reception. I never made it back!

I was involved in a near-fatal automobile accident, a head-on collision in our Volkswagen Beetle with a pickup truck. My right leg was broken in five places: the fibula in two places, tibia in two places, and my ankle! I had to be cut out of the car. I remember lying on the ground surrounded by people and two girls eating popcorn and laughing.

It was surreal! I had a comminuted fracture, and I was incapacitated for almost three years.

Nine operations, nineteen screws, two metal plates, skin grafts, crutches, and pain, pain, pain! The doctor placed gauze in my leg wound, let it dry, then slowly pulled it out to remove the dead skin. This was necessary for my leg to begin to heal, but the pain was unbearable!

The doctor gave me two options: (1) remove the broken bones which would leave my leg an inch and a half short; or (2) add plates and screws which could lead to infections, but my leg would be the normal length. I chose option two! For the first time in our union, Maséqua found herself fighting battles alone.

I had to learn how to walk with crutches and a full leg cast for a year, then a half cast, and then a boot with a cane and therapy for almost three years. I also had to self-administer my antibiotics with an IV once a day.

During my recovery from the car accident, Helen Mason, founder of the Black Theatre Troupe, hired Maséqua as interim artistic director of the theatre. She ran the theatre during the day, and she took a job at a convenience store at night. A show she produced and directed, the musical *Ain't Misbehavin'*, went on the road. She instantly became the sole breadwinner and sole parent of our two sons in a city we had just relocated to one year before until I could literally get back on my feet again. When I look back, I'm not sure how she got through it.

Our Volkswagen after my crash

In 1974, Maséqua had graduated from Kennedy-King College with a double AA degree in theatre and nursing. Maséqua being a graduate and registered nurse came in handy for the family!

With our sons growing up, inevitably, Nurse Maséqua would be called into action on several occasions.

While in Phoenix, our eldest son, Babatunde, broke his collarbone (twice) and Tacuma broke his wrist. In one particularly eventful motorcycle escapade in California, they both broke their right foot simultaneously!

It was an intense time for our family and a humbling time for me. Ironically, in 1985, in Flagstaff, Arizona, Maséqua played a nurse in the film, *Zoo Gang*, starring Jason Gedrick and Ben Vereen. She wore her nursing school uniform to the audition, and maybe that was a plus.

It was the first time I felt small. The world went on without me, and nothing stopped. It was also a time of revelations. Living with the majority being Caucasians in Phoenix brought me to the realization that people are all fundamentally the same. I became more tolerant by coming to understand that ignorance is just the state of where people are. I tried not to hold it against them. I came to believe we should all leave the planet a better place than we found it. Being forced to sit down and be still became a time of reinvention for me. It took almost a year before I returned to managing the Phoenix Black Theatre Troupe, even though I remained on crutches.

Maséqua's reputation was growing in Arizona as an actress, director, and producer. She was hired to present a performance of her one-woman show, *Through the Eyes of Women*, at a conference addressing homeless and battered women in the '90s. The *"Take Back the Night"* conference was held at the newly built National YWCA of The USA Leadership Development Center, a multi-million-dollar state-of-the-art training facility.

When Blackness was Golden

Maséqua arranged for us to tour the facility to consider renting it to produce a show. We decided to produce a comedy show featuring Robert Townsend, David Spade, and the late Jesse Aragon. It was fantastic!

While we were touring the facility, the director Deloris Brinkley told us they were searching for an audio-visual technology director. At Maséqua's insistence, I reluctantly applied.

A few days before my interview, I read an article in the Arizona Republic newspaper about Richard Altman, the person with whom I would be interviewing for the position. Richard was opening a hologram exhibit at a local museum, and I decided to attend. When my interview came around, I was still walking with a cane, but I left it in the car during my interview.

Throughout the interview, we talked more about his exhibit than my background! The interview took place in the tech booth of the 500-seat multipurpose room. There was a video projector, two reel to reel tape recorders, slide projectors (three-quarter inches) and two (one-half inch) video tape machines. Since I had worked with this type of equipment in my technology-driven productions, I deduced the job would be a piece of cake!

YWCA of the USA Leadership Development Center in Phoenix

I was hired to run this state-of-the-art training and media center and hit the ground running, producing a weekly cable TV show at the facility. On my first day, they took me on a full facility tour. Had I seen the entire facility, I would have been more reluctant to take the position! The part of the facility I did not see during the interview included a full multi-camera TV studio, satellite uplink and downlink, a photo/multimedia center with a darkroom as well as an audio recording studio. In six weeks, I read every manual and learned to work all the major equipment, some of which I had never even seen before showing up to work the first day.

The Leadership Development Center staff was familiar with Maséqua's work from her performances with the YWCA. Eventually, she was brought in as a consultant, and we were again doing one of the things we do best — work together.

With Maséqua working as a creative consultant to the Phoenix YWCA, we produced *"It's OK to Say No Way,"* an award-winning rap video written by Chicagoan Michael "Mangelo" Pugh, which dealt with teen pregnancy prevention. The video earned first-place awards from the International Television Association and the Arizona Health Association.

I also produced and directed *"Follow Your Dreams,"* a music video covering non-traditional careers for girls for the Arizona Board of Education, which earned a second-place award from the National Association of Vocational Educators. For the Maricopa County Medical Center, Maséqua wrote, produced, directed, and conducted a statewide tour of *Give Life A Chance*, a musical production centered on the importance of prenatal care for teenage mothers and young adults.

Many other productions followed, including *The Height of Dedication*, a documentary on civil rights activist Dr. Dorothy Height, which won a merit award from the International Television Association; *"Get Out The Vote"* commercials produced in English and Spanish for the Women's Vote Project in Washington, DC; and *"The Young Women's Employment Training Project,"* produced for the U.S. Dept. of Labor in Boston, MA, and Miami, FL.

The Leadership Development Center was owned by the National YWCA, headquartered in Manhattan, New York. As a member of the national staff, I was required to attend monthly meetings in New York, which also gave me an opportunity to spend a lot of time seeing theatre on and off Broadway.

During one of my many visits, I caught a taxi to see a play on Broadway. I was picked up by a Black man who wore thick glasses, and his hair was long, wild, and ungroomed.

He was a bit strange! As we sped toward Lower Manhattan, he nearly hit a Hispanic couple that was crossing the street. The couple cursed the driver in their language.

He slammed on his brakes, jumped out of the taxi, beat up the man, and pushed his wife to the ground as I sat in the back seat in complete shock! The crazed driver finally got back in the taxi and sped off with me still in the back seat! I politely asked the driver to drop me off at the next corner. I could make it to the theatre on foot, and it would be a lot less stressful!

Harold Vick, a jazz saxophonist and flautist, became a dear friend. Harold released several albums as band leader during the 1960s and '70s and worked with Jack McDuff, Jimmy McGriff, and Shirley Scott. He also played with Nat Adderley, Aretha Franklin, Dizzy Gillespie, Mercer Ellington, Sarah Vaughan, Billy Taylor, Donald Byrd, and Jimmy Smith. Harold Vick played saxophone in films such as Stardust Memories, Cotton Club, Spike Lee's School Daze, and he was featured on the soundtrack for *She's Gotta Have It.* Harold was musical director and composer for several documentaries I produced while at the Leadership Development Center, including *It's OK to Say No Way* and *The Height of Dedication.* The documentary was narrated by Gloria Foster and included interviews with Lena Horne, Jesse Jackson, and J. Richard Munro, former chairman and chief executive officer of Time Inc. The soundtrack was recorded at the studio of percussionist, songwriter, musical arranger, and record producer Ralph McDonald in New York.

Gloria Foster, who played the oracle in *The Matrix* and *The Matrix Reloaded* films, was the first major celebrity I directed, and I must admit I was intimidated — so much so that I really didn't direct her and ended up not liking her narration. I decided I would never let that happen again. A few years later, when I directed James Earl Jones, I probably pushed him more than I should have because of that experience.

I also produced a video, *The Role of a Judge in a Jury Trial*, for the Arizona Supreme Court and *"Renaissance,"* a public service announcement for the Phoenix Black Theatre Troupe. It won the Gold Nugget Award from the American Advertising Association.

Our theatrical productions also never stopped. Maséqua was selected as Artist in Residence with the Arizona Commission on the Arts and traveled the state performing and teaching communication skills and self-esteem through the arts. In addition, she was director and tour manager for the Black Theatre Troupe's production of Fats Waller's musical, *Ain't Misbehavin'*, which traveled the entire state of Arizona. The production assisted the theatre's fundraising efforts to purchase a new facility.

In 1988, the Phoenix Ladies of Distinction awarded Maséqua the Excellence in Arts Award.

When our eldest son Babatunde graduated from high school, he wanted to pursue his acting career in Los Angeles. So, I resigned from the Leadership Development Center with a glowing recommendation letter from Dr. Gwendolyn Baker, the National Executive Director of the YWCA of USA, and we packed up the family and headed to L.A.!

National Board YWCA of the U.S.A.

726 Broadway
New York, NY 10003
212-614-2700
Cable: Emissarius, NY

December 5, 1988

Mr. Penon Rami
Production Specialist
YWCA of the U.S.A.
Leadership Development Center
9440 North 25th Avenue
Phoenix, Arizona 85021

Dear Penon:

It will be hard for us to imagine Phoenix, the LDC and the Media Center without you. Your spirit, creativity, flexibility, energy and professionalism stand out in our minds as we think of you. The way you have involved your talented family in your endeavors has also been a special gift to us. Your linkage with the larger technical and creative community in multiple locations has also been a distinct asset for the national movement.

The list of some thirty productions either produced or directed by you in the last few years is most impressive. Many of these stand out as spectacular creations! What a legacy you are leaving the entire nation in "The Height of Dedication! How memorable to young and old is "It's Okay to Say No Way"! Will you ever forget your two triennial conventions in San Jose and Chicago, or the World Council?

We have deep respect and admiration for you! We hold you in the highest esteem! We count it a rare privilege to have been associated with you!

Every good thing imaginable is wished for you. We know we are going to be hearing glowing reports about you from the west coast media community.

We are appreciative of your desire to continue to work with us in future YWCA undertakings.

The entire National Board and staff join me in the fondest of farewells.

Sincerely,

Gwendolyn Calvert Baker
National Executive Director

GCB:vl

Affiliated with the World YWCA
...in the struggle for peace and justice, freedom and dignity for all people

Chapter Twelve: Look Out, Los Angeles

For years, we had considered a move to Los Angeles. During the filming of *Mahogany*, Berry Gordy suggested I consider moving to the West Coast. At the time, however, I was committed to Chicago. Since Berry didn't make me a specific job offer, I wasn't motivated. It was our eldest son Babatunde's desire to pursue an acting career that prompted our eventual move to L.A. following his high school graduation.

After getting the family settled in L.A., I returned to Phoenix as a consultant for the YWCA Leadership Development Center while they searched for my replacement.

When I completed the consultancy, I returned to L.A. I decided to anchor the family by finding a job there. Back then, there were want ads in most major newspapers. I saw an advertisement for an audio-visual specialist at Cedars-Sinai Medical Center and applied. I was invited to interview and met with the department manager. I also met with the head of the department who, in the middle of the interview, left the room without saying a word and never came back. When I returned home, I told Maséqua about the interview and said, "I guess I didn't get that one!" However, a few days later, I was offered the position. I was told it was the recommendation from Dr. Baker that convinced them I was the right person for the job.

One of my first assignments was videotaping and editing a series of videos covering the work of Dr. David Ho, a resident in internal medicine at Cedars-Sinai in 1981 when he encountered some of the first reported cases of what was later identified as AIDS. I shot and edited the early videos of his work. I was nervous going into the surgery suites and patient rooms, not knowing how safe I would be.

Maséqua got busy right away and was cast in a production of *One Last Look*, directed by Ed Cambridge at Marla Gibbs Crossroads Theatre. Whitman Mayo, the academy director at Crossroads who played Grady in *Sanford and Son*, was so impressed with Maséqua that he offered her a job teaching acting classes. I submitted my resume to the academy as well. I received a call from Whitman, and he scheduled a time for me to meet with Marla. After reviewing my resume, they said they didn't want to offer me a teaching position, but because of my administrative background, they wanted to offer me the position of executive director since Marla's daughter, Angela, was leaving the position.

Whitman and I had met in the early seventies when we were in New York, and he was talent coordinator at the New Lafayette Theatre in Harlem. During the auditions for Sanford and Son, Whitman took some of their actors to LA to audition. The producers cast Whitman instead and sent the other actors back to New York. I resigned my position at Cedars and joined Maséqua, Marla, and Whitman at Crossroads!

Marla had purchased the multimillion-dollar Crossroads complex the last year of her television show, 227, with the expectation of paying for it with the syndication bonus she was to receive. However, the show was canceled before the studio was obligated to pay her the bonus. The Crossroads Academy complex, which I soon renamed the Vision Complex, included a 1,200-seat theatre, a ninety-nine-seat theatre, a banquet facility, classrooms, and retail property.

At the same time, Marla was also trying to maintain her Memory Lane night club that was a cash cow. When she eliminated the training academy due to lack of income, Maséqua offered to take charge. She was elevated to Academy director and director of the Summer Youth Institute. Enrollment soared.

When Blackness was Golden

Instead of being shut down, the staff was increased. Maséqua also developed a four-week producer-casting directors' master series featuring Reuben Cannon.

Under my new management, we increased activities and income in the large theatre by producing concerts featuring Nancy Wilson, the Winans, Stevie Wonder, the Duke Ellington Orchestra, Robert Townsend, Eddie Griffin, Gerald Albright, and others. It was in the ninety-nine-seat Crossroads Theatre that Maséqua produced and I directed Miss Dessa, a romantic comedy written by Chicagoan Shirley Hardy who also penned *Where is the Pride, What is the Joy*, which I directed at X-BAG.

The play netted eight NAACP Theatre awards, including Best Producer for Maséqua and Best Director for me. Our first Hollywood award show and we won big!

I also contacted the film studios and solicited their using the facility to host screenings of films they were preparing to premiere, as fundraisers for the Vision Complex. One film was *A Rage in Harlem*, directed by Bill Duke and starring Gregory Hines, Forest Whitaker, Danny Glover, and Robin Givens. We produced the first series of African-American red carpet feature film premieres in a Black-owned theatre, including *Living Large, James Brown the Man and His Music*, and *The Josephine Baker Story*.

A who's who of Black Hollywood was in attendance! Denzel Washington, Wesley Snipes, Luther Vandross, Robert Townsend, Keenen Ivory Wayans, Bill Duke, Gregory Hines, Forest Whitaker, Danny Glover, Robin Givens, and Little Richard were all in the audience. As executive producer of the events, I addressed the star-studded crowd. In the middle of my speech, Little Richard entered with four young male escorts.

I stopped mid-speech and suggested the audience acknowledge Little Richard, then continued my speech after his entourage was seated. He wasn't stealing my moment!

Although I had a great time at Vision, it was too much work and expensive to maintain.

It was also during this time that The Hollywood Reporter entertainment magazine published an article stating that Black people didn't want to see films like Robert Townsend's *Five Heartbeats* but preferred movies like *Boyz n the Hood*. Disturbed by the published report, Robert asked me to accompany him to Washington, DC, and meet with Reverend Jesse Jackson to solicit his support.

We flew into DC and met Jesse at a health club. He greeted us warmly and stated he would meet us later for dinner. That evening, we met at an Italian restaurant, and it was like a scene from *The Godfather*. People kept coming up to the table to greet Jesse and "kiss his ring."

I explained our desire to create a campaign surrounding the film. As we enjoyed a wonderful dinner, Jesse blurted out, "You have to pay the piper!" He was implying that if we wanted him to be the spokesman for the protest, he had to be paid! As we headed back to the hotel, Robert and I laughed at the matter-of-fact way Reverend Jackson made his request.

At the restaurant before Jesse arrived, then-Senator Joe Biden came over to our table to tell Robert he was a fan and loved his work. When I returned to Los Angeles, we took out an ad in The Hollywood Reporter identifying prominent people supporting the film. Maya Angelou and Spike Lee were among over one hundred celebrities that signed the ad.

When Blackness was Golden

By 1991, I had become extremely proficient with computers.

Our time in Phoenix had opened me up to this new technology, and we purchased our first Hewlett-Packard laptops. Whitman Mayo and his wife Gail had become Maséqua's and my close friends. Whitman suggested I buy his black and white Macintosh classic computer because he was purchasing a new one. When I asked why, Whitman replied, "Once you go Mac, you never go back!" And he was right! I have worked on a Mac for more than thirty years now, and the PC is not even close in ease of use and care.

My work at the Vision Theatre Complex, producing and managing events, was exhausting and unending. There were ongoing activities seven days a week and ten to twelve hours a day. There was no light at the end of the tunnel, so I resigned and moved on.

A few days after I decided to depart from the Vision Theatre Complex, the 1992 Los Angeles riots began after a jury acquitted four officers of the Los Angeles Police charged with using excessive force in the beating of Rodney King. We stood outside the theatre complex as the neighborhood burned. The people in the community protected the complex from rioters and looters.

Our activities in L.A. continued with Maséqua producing and me directing the NAACP Sixth Annual Theatre Awards, which Maséqua negotiated to be held at the Directors Guild of America in their beautiful theatre. James Earl Jones was presented with a lifetime achievement award and, when he could not attend the event, I directed the shoot of his acceptance speech. We shot the footage at the Samuel French Bookstore on Sunset Boulevard.

During this period, I also helped Maséqua develop another version of her one-woman show titled, *Through the Eyes of*

Women, which was mounted at the Complex Theatre in Hollywood on Santa Monica Boulevard. I directed the show, which opened to rave reviews.

Robert Townsend purchased the building that housed the Hollywood Professional School at 8033 West Sunset Boulevard in 1990 and renamed it Tinsel Townsend Studios. Robert asked me to assist as a script reader and to direct staged readings of selective projects. I also wrote a creative plan for the theatre which was planned to be remodeled. Unfortunately, the facility toppled during the North Ridge earthquake, putting a stop to that dream.

Gladys Knight

In Los Angeles, Maséqua had secured recognition as a creative writer, producer, and teacher. Reuben Cannon recruited her as company manager for a play starring Gladys Knight, titled *Madame Lily,* that was in preproduction for a national tour.

The production was written by Ron Milner and produced by Gladys's ex-husband, Barry Hankerson, a self-proclaimed Detroit gangster. Hankerson had been a television producer and a politician in Detroit, Michigan. He managed the Winans, R. Kelly and Public Announcement, and R&B singer Aaliyah until her death on August 25, 2001, in a plane crash in the Bahamas. In addition, Hankerson managed Toni Braxton.

When Blackness was Golden

David Peaston, Gladys Knight, and Dorian Harewood in *Madame Lily*

The play also starred Dorian Harewood and David Peaston. As the producers were searching for a director, Maséqua recommended me for the job. At the time, Barry and Ron didn't know we were married. I had directed The Monster, Ron Milner's first major theatrical production at the Southside Center of The Performing Arts in 1969, so in the beginning we were pleased to re-connect! Auditions and rehearsals were held in Los Angeles, but directing the production turned out to be my worst theatrical experience and my best.

I have always loved Gladys as an entertainer, so to be the only person in the rehearsal at her home while she sang was an experience I will never forget! I also worked with her family during that time. Her daughter Kenya, her sons Jimmy (deceased) and Shanga, and Glady's brother, Bubba, were all great to work with, but Barry Hankerson was another story! While we were on the road, one of the female leads in the cast complained to me when she discovered she had an adjoining hotel room with Barry, and the inner door was unlocked and open! The script was still being written when we started rehearsal. Gladys, Dorian, and David all had engagements that would not allow for them to be at rehearsals at the same time until two weeks before we opened in Chicago. Barry's son, Jomo, was put in charge of the tour, but Barry didn't provide enough money to cover the cost.

As we were preparing for the tour in Los Angeles and it was announced Chicago would be our first stop, I requested family friend and then president of Kennedy-King College, Dr. Harold Pates, allow us to use their theatre for rehearsals prior to our opening at the Arie Crown Theatre. In exchange, we would allow them to use our dress rehearsal as a fundraiser for the college. He agreed. When Barry didn't like the set that was built in Detroit and shipped to Kennedy King, he instructed the set designer to hire students to build a new set and use the wood and materials at the school as needed. After it was completed, Barry refused to reimburse the college. Gladys paid for it so her name would not be tarnished.

The directing experience was also miserable at times. I would direct a scene, and Barry or Ron would fly in days later and change what I had done. The play was being written until opening night at the Arie Crown Theatre at McCormick Place, and then the show traveled to the Fox Theatre in Atlanta. When we completed the Atlanta run, I returned to L.A. while the show went on to Baltimore.

I'd had enough! Back in Los Angeles, I received a call from Maséqua informing me that Barry had run out of cash and decided to cancel the tour after Baltimore.

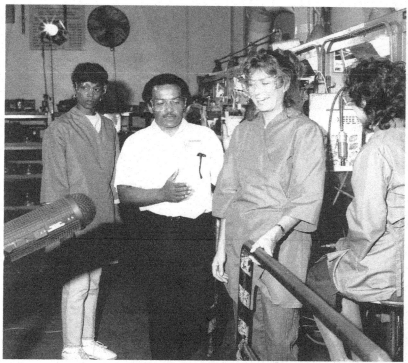

Directing *Get Out the Vote* commercial in Los Angeles. Produced for the Women's Vote Project, Washington, D.C.

The following day, I received a telephone call from Cedars-Sinai Medical Center which determined the next eight years of our lives.

Photo by Michael Sexton for *AV Multimedia Magazine*

Chapter Thirteen: The Hospital to the Stars

The phone call I received was from the head of Human Resources at Cedars-Sinai Medical Center in Beverly Hills, California, to request I return as the head of their Medical Media Department. I wasn't pursuing a full-time job at the time, but they said since I had done such a wonderful job when I worked for them as the audio-visual specialist, they offered me the position before it was publicly posted.

Maséqua and I were having fun with a variety of exciting entertainment projects, and I wanted to see how far that could take us. So, when they asked me what it would take for me to come on board, I quoted an amount of money I thought they would reject, but they said OK. The interesting thing is that the Medical Center's rabbi told me that if I had applied for the job, I probably never would have gotten it.

For the next eight years, I managed the Medical Media and Conference Services Department at the Medical Center. For my efforts, I was presented with the center's President's Award for designing the interactive patient and staff education TV system and was featured on the cover of AV Video Multimedia Producer magazine.

During my tenure there, I was responsible for managing and supervising the video, computer graphic, photography, illustration, and conference services/audio visual units for a world-class, tertiary, acute care, teaching medical center.

My additional responsibilities included supervision and design of various projection and closed-circuit systems for the Medical Center as well as the in-house interactive TV system and programming of six in-house closed-circuit TV channels. I also produced over 200 medical industrial films on topics ranging from open heart surgery to birthing instruction.

While working at Cedars-Sinai, I had the opportunity to work with Steven Spielberg, Monty Hall, Hal David, James Garner, George Burns, Kirk Douglas, Michael Douglas, Angela Bassett, Ed McMahon, Dr. Lynn Masterson, Dr. Keith Black, Dr. David Ho, Wolfgang Puck, Tony Orlando, and some of the best doctors and nurses in the world.

Directing the late Ed McMahon at Cedars-Sinai Medical Center

Jerk Chicken and Rum Punch at Denzel's House

Dr. Rickey Hendrix, one of the doctors I met at Cedars, was also an aspiring filmmaker. An OB-GYN by profession, Rickey had taken off from his practice to attend the American Film Institute to follow his dream. His relationship with stars whose babies he had delivered put him in close proximity to his true desire to make movies. Rickey even had the opportunity to shoot the behind-the-scenes documentaries for *Devil in A Blue Dress* and *The Preacher's Wife*, both of which starred Denzel Washington.

When Blackness was Golden

In the summer of 1994, Rickey called to ask if I wanted to attend a barbeque at Denzel Washington's house for the Fourth of July. Of course, I said yes. The jerk chicken and rum punch were the bomb! There were only a few of us there. Rickey and I, Denzel and his wife Pauletta, Laurence Fishburne, Victoria Dillard, and casting director and producer Reuben Cannon, whom I had met in the early eighties when we worked in Chicago on the television movie, Welcome to Success.

Reuben had grown up in Harold Ickes projects and had started working in Hollywood in the mailroom. Cannon was the first Black casting director in Hollywood; he was the head of television casting for Warner Brothers from 1977 to 1978 when he started his own casting agency—Reuben Cannon & Associates. He has been credited with launching the careers of many of today's major film and television stars, including Oprah, Whoopi, and Danny Glover.

Reuben also worked as a producer of many of Tyler Perry's television shows and movies.

I had a great time, and, like I said earlier, the rum punch and jerk chicken Denzel made was the fire! It was wonderful just talking about everything but the entertainment business and to spend time with these men and woman without having to worry about flossing. No one wanted anything from each other but a relaxing good time. The following January (1994), the Northridge earthquake destroyed Denzel's house in Toluca Lake, California, close to the Hollywood Hills. The homes of Gladys Knight, Warren Beatty, Walter Matthau and Jack Nicholson were also seriously damaged.

One day I received a phone call from the head of nursing to personally install an 8mm film projector in a patient's room and not assign it to my staff. When I went to the room, I saw why.

The patient was Sammy Davis Jr.! Sammy was being treated for throat cancer and wanted to watch his old movies. I spent as much time with him during his last days as I was allowed and thanked him for his support of the Umoja Black Student Center during the student movement in Chicago. Sammy passed away after a nine-month battle with throat cancer in May 1990. Another one of my full circle events!

Then trouble struck our family again.

Chapter Fourteen: My Parents' Illness

My mother was diagnosed with adult-onset diabetes, and the family was informed her leg had become infected and needed to be amputated. My eighty-year-old father became her full-time caregiver. Shortly thereafter, he was diagnosed with prostate cancer when two tumors were discovered on his spine. He soon became paralyzed and was told he would never walk again. Maséqua and I began traveling back and forth from Los Angeles to Chicago every few weeks for over two years to assist with their care as much as we could from afar. Even though the doctors told my father he would never walk again, he miraculously was able to overcome his paralysis and walk again!

When I went to visit him, he was sitting in his wheelchair. We must have sat there for about an hour, talking and catching up, when he got up out of his chair and walked across the room! I almost had a heart attack! He had kept his walking a secret. He said he noticed his toe move. He got a karate belt and started exercising his legs until he could stand. After he started walking again, he installed parquet floors in his condo and did the woodwork before another tumor developed on his spine and he became paralyzed again.

During those difficult days of illness, Maséqua, my sister Barbara, and I took on the responsibility for their care. We took turns traveling to Chicago every few weeks to take care of my parents, cleaning, paying their bills, cooking, and taking them to doctor's visits.

During this challenging time, I was featured on the cover of *AV Video Multimedia Producer* magazine (November 1999) for designing the interactive television system for Cedars-Sinai Medical Center.

AV Video Multimedia Producer magazine cover, November 1999

When Blackness was Golden

My father's paralysis returned, so our travels back to Chicago became more intense. My mother and father required constant care. Both were moved into the same nursing home but different rooms because my father didn't want my mother to see him suffer.

At eighty-four, he refused pain medication because, as he said, "I don't want to become addicted!" I tried to get him to try marijuana for pain management, but he refused. The doctor ultimately gave him a pain patch.

When I returned to L.A., I received a call from Arup, a British multinational professional services firm with offices in eighty countries, providing engineering, architecture, design, planning, project management, and consulting services for all aspects of the building environment. I was offered a position to head their audio-visual design division, and I accepted the six-figure position. My first major project was the design of the new AV system for Los Angeles International Airport.

Four weeks later, I returned to Chicago because my father's health was continuing to fail. I stayed with him for a week, and I told my father I had to go back to Los Angeles to follow-up on the Arup projects. I told him I would return in two weeks. "I may not be here when you return," Dad said. "Don't you die on me!" I replied.

The night I returned to Chicago—within two weeks, as promised—I went to the nursing home to visit my father and my mom. He told me to call my sister and have her come to Chicago that night. She rushed to get a flight from Philly. When Barbara arrived at Midway Airport that same night, I picked her up and we headed directly to the nursing home.

We sat talking with Dad for a few hours, and he suggested we go home and get some sleep. The following morning, we got a call from the nursing home and were told he was nonresponsive.

My sister and I immediately went to the nursing home and found him in a semiconscious state. We both held his hands until he took his last breath.

Planning Dad's funeral was eye-opening and depressing. The funeral homes try to sell you on everything. I was also surprised that they rent everything from coffins to clothes for the deceased to wear. My father enjoyed the Blues, so our good friend, three-time Grammy nominee Billy Branch, agreed to play at the funeral.

After my father passed, we asked our mother if she wanted to move to L.A. with me or Philadelphia with my sister. Mom decided she would move with Barbara to Philly.

I returned to L.A. to my job at Arup, but I was devastated by my father's death. Even though I tried, I could not work my way into the new job. I could not focus. I realized later it was depression. After five months at Arup, I called Maséqua and told her I wanted to quit. Supportive as usual, she said it was up to me, and we would make it regardless of my decision. So, I resigned and joined Maséqua's company!

When Blackness was Golden

Maséqua and I refocused our union as equal business partners and not just colleagues. Our lives have been so dynamic—the sense of change—we set about creating and producing the well-received *"Spotlight on Actors Night,"* at the Mixed Nuts Comedy Club. During our last couple of years in L.A., we had taken *You Decide*, a dramatized interactive radio talk show, from conception to development. Maséqua and I hosted the show which aired on KPFK Pacifica radio station in L.A. and the American Radio Network globally. In addition, under the auspices of Maséqua Myers and Associates, we developed a brilliantly written and researched four-part documentary for PBS titled *The Effect of Ethnicity, Culture and Race on Mental Health*. The project was never completed due to the 9-11 attack on the World Trade Center, and the PBS funds were shifted to other priorities.

When our wedding anniversary came around, we decided it was time to take a serious break, so off to Maui we went! The island of Maui—the second largest of the Hawaiian islands and the seventeenth largest island in the United States—is a great place for relaxation. We stayed at the beautiful Royal Lahaina Resort on Kaanapali Beach, which had been named one of the best beaches in the world. Our beachfront cottage was amazing, and we enjoyed all the island had to offer. Rejuvenated, we returned to L.A. with the intention of producing a national acting competition.

Since my mother's health was failing, we decided to move back to Chicago. Maséqua's mom was also up in age, so our staying in Chicago would be good for her as well. We had rented their condo to what became the tenant from hell, and we needed to have them evicted and repair the damage that was done to the condo.

WHAT HAPPENED TO MY SOUTH SIDE?

One of the disappointing things about returning to Chicago for me was that most of the places I lived and remembered as a child had been destroyed! Where my grandmother lived—where my family lived—most entertainment venues and restaurants had become victims of urban renewal, what we referred to as "urban removal and gentrification." It is an eerie feeling to drive through a neighborhood where you grew up and not see one structure standing that was special to you, but that is what happened to most of the Black communities on the South Side of Chicago. What is clear is the city was so determined to re-claim the valuable land where poor Black folks lived on the South Side that it was necessary to tear down the old buildings to get rid of all the residents and ensure other poor folks didn't move in! Further, the new structures that have taken their place are not as well-built or sturdy, and most are smaller. While riding the elevator train from Sixty-Third Street and Cottage Grove to Downtown, I was motivated to write this:

What Happened to My South Side?

What happened to the South Side
once the pride of Black Chicago?
It has been over twenty years!
What happened to the people?
No longer Black and Proud
What happened to Woodlawn, Englewood,
South Shore, Chatham, Auburn Gresham,
and the low end?
My memories are fading; the landmarks are
no more!
No more grandma's house or the place of my
birth.
No more Stateway Gardens or Robert Taylor
Homes.

When Blackness was Golden

Too many vacant lots, vacant faces, and vacant minds.
We used to have a pep in our steps and a glide in our stride
Now our pants are sagging, and our people are dragging.
Was it drugs? The man? A devious plan?
How did we go so high to sink so low?
There was a time when the L train ride from 63rd to Howard was an adventure of discovery.
Looking out the window on the north bound train I search for places where life once bustled by!
Now all I see are empty lots and lost souls waiting to die.
What happened to the South Side? 47th, Garfield, 63rd and 79th?
People claim Bronzeville is returning! But I wonder to what?
Politicians promised the housing projects would be replaced, but when, with what and for who?
What happened to our children who can no longer dream?
What has happened to our children whose lives seem to have no meaning!
The hope of our people lies in the strength and minds of the young! Despite everything, they keep on coming on strong. We must win!

Pemon Rami 2003

Chapter Fifteen: Trinidad, Tobago and Brazil

In 2002, I received a call from Robert Townsend asking if I could accompany him to Trinidad and Tobago to meet with representatives of the government regarding developing a plan to expand their film and television industry. At first, I said no because we were in the middle of negotiations with XM satellite for the syndication of our You Decide! radio show, and Trinidad and Tobago were not on my "bucket list."

Maséqua once again stressed the importance of the opportunity and convinced me to go, so I was off on another adventure.

When I arrived at Piarco Airport in Trinidad, the first thing that stood out to me was the pictures of all the Black government officials on the walls. As a guest of the government, we received the royal treatment! A special envoy met us at the plane and escorted us through customs.

The Upside-Down Hilton Hotel commands views of Port of Spain overlooking the Queen's Park Savannah. It's called the Upside-Down Hotel because you take the elevator down to the higher-numbered floors.

Our personal driver and tour guide assigned to us by the government, Tony Poyer, was wonderful and well-versed on the island's history, culture, and traditions.

The objective of our first visit was to scout locations for filming and meet with government officials and production companies. We flew by helicopter over the countryside and over the Caribbean Sea to the smaller island, Tobago.

After a driving tour around Tobago and the countryside, we took

When Blackness was Golden

a yacht around Trinidad seeing the island from every possible angle. While on the island of Tobago, we stayed at the beautiful Tobago Hilton.

Artwork by Boscoe Holder, Trinidad and Tobago's leading contemporary painter, adorned the hotel. Boscoe, the brother of Geoffrey Holder, was also a celebrated international designer, visual artist, dancer, choreographer, and musician.

The trip to Trinidad and Tobago was a fruitful start. We were invited to return in a few months following my development of the preliminary report. Our second trip to Trinidad was to attend Carnival and to meet with Trinidad and Tobago's top talent pool. Maséqua joined me in Trinidad for Carnival, which is celebrated on the Monday and Tuesday before the Catholic holiday, Ash Wednesday.

Carnival in Trinidad Photo credit: Maséqua

Carnival in Trinidad and Tobago are the most significant events on the islands, with numerous other cultural activities

during the weeks leading up to the street parades on Lundi Gras (Monday) and Mardi Gras (Tuesday). It is said that if the islanders are not celebrating Carnival, then they are preparing for it, while reminiscing about the past year's festival.

Soca, Trinidadian popular music that developed in the 1970s, is the most celebrated type of music during Carnival. However, Soca gets very little play outside of the Carnival season. Costumes, steel drums, stick fighting, and limbo competitions are also important components of the festival. I should also mention filmmakers Horace Ove, Danielle Dieffenthaller, artist Leroy Clark, and singers Pat Bishop and the Mighty Sparrow, a few of the wonderful and super talented people we had the opportunity to spend time with. Experiencing Carnival in Trinidad is hard to explain.

With Robert Townsend in Trinidad

When Blackness was Golden

The music, the processionals, the costumes, and the beautiful people have been embedded in my mind forever. Following Carnival and days of recovery, we met with government officials, artists, and creative organizations to develop an extensive business plan including a series of productions Robert Townsend could produce in Trinidad and Tobago, and we submitted the ideas to TIDCO, the Tourism and Industrial Development Company.

Our original assumption was that the Trinidad government was going to provide funding to produce the series of films and television shows. However, it turned out the Trinidadian government really wanted Robert to provide funding or move some of his production activities to Trinidad and Tobago. Regrettably, that project never moved forward.

Maséqua and I stayed in Trinidad for a few extra weeks and had a wonderful time exploring the island. We were very tempted to relocate to Trinidad or Tobago.

With Maséqua at El Cerro del Aripo, the highest point in Trinidad

Hollywood Squares

Before we departed for Trinidad, I received a call from *Hollywood Squares* to be a guest contestant on the show. *Hollywood Squares* was one of Maséqua's favorite TV shows, and I tried to secretly register her to be on the show. When I called the show, I was told I could not call for someone else, but I could apply and add her name as a suggested contestant. We both auditioned and were subsequently selected as prospective contestants. When they called to invite me to appear on the show, I told them I was leaving the country and could not return to L.A. The show's producer told me he understood and to call them when I returned to the States.

When we returned to the States, I called the producer and was invited to appear as a contestant. The celebrities on the show included Lou Rawls, Martin Mull, Sherri Shepherd, Charo, Hattie Winston, and Lenny Clark. I won the first game, and the opposing contestant (champion) won the second game. For the third game, each of us answered all our questions correctly. Because the current champion went first, it gave her an advantage, and she was able to win with five squares. I went home with $1,000. I had a great time, and I was included, along with Lou Rawls, in the closing credits. Maséqua and our two sons attended the taping. Even though Maséqua was selected for the contestant list, she never appeared on the show.

Salvador Bahia and Rio de Janeiro, Brazil

Later that summer, we were commissioned to travel to Salvador Bahia and Rio de Janeiro, Brazil, to document the African Brazilian Connection. The African heritage tour organized by Dr. Anderson Thompson traced the African roots of Brazil.

When Blackness was Golden

We produced the travelogue to shed light on African Brazilian culture, i.e., ways of being, ways of thinking, ways of acting. Dr. Anderson Thompson, professor at Northeastern Illinois University Center for Inner City Studies, taught Brazilian culture ethos for decades in Chicago, and many students were well-versed in Brazilian cultural variables and codifications.

We flew to Brazil on TAM Airlines headquartered in São Paulo. TAM Airlines flies to various destinations in South America, North America, and Europe. When we were at the ticket counter checking in, we mentioned we would be celebrating our anniversary while in Brazil. The ticket agents congratulated us, then offered to upgrade us to first class for a small fee. We agreed and were amused at the shock of the other people traveling with us as they passed us in first class on their way to coach. Unfortunately, we could not get the same offer coming back!

Salvador da Bahia is the largest city on the northeast coast of Brazil and the capital of the northeastern Brazilian state of Bahia. Salvador is also known as the Black State of Brazil. The first colonial capital of Brazil, the city is one of the oldest in the New World.

Digue dos Torrero Park in Salvador da Bahia in Brazil, which is famous for Orisha Lake and statues of Orisha gods Photo credit: Maséqua

Over eighty percent of the population claim some African ancestry. African influences permeate Brazilian society in every visible way, including music, cuisine, spiritual beliefs, and dance. Their culture also reflects African roots and resistance to enslavement. Organizations like Irmande da Boa Morte and the House of Gandhi give testimony to the organized efforts of African Brazilians to hold on to their identity and culture. Racism in Brazil is on a different level of disgusting. The week we arrived, all dark-skinned employees at one of their banks were fired and replaced with white or light-complected Brazilians.

Dancing with the Sons of Gandhi at the House of Gandhi Photo credit: Maséqua

The Sons of Gandhi was founded in 1948 following Gandhi's murder. Gandhi is still an inspiration to the oppressed Afro-Brazilians, who are fighting for equality through peaceful means.

Brazil's Mixed-Race Designations
By Dr. Anderson Thompson

Portuguese	English	Hair	Skin
Branco	White	Straight/wavy	White
Moreno		Straight/wavy	Sun Burnt/white
Mulato	Light Bright	Crisp/curly	Darker than Moreno
Amerelo	Yellow		
Chulo		Crisp/rolled	Burnt sugar
Creolo		Fine/wavy	Dark as Chulo
Cabo Verde		Straight	
Pardo			Brown
Negro	Black		Black
Preto	Black	Coil spring	Black

Playing conga as Maséqua plays the shakers in a music and instrument workshop at the Bahia Othon Palace in Salvador da Bahia, Brazil

While Maséqua and I were shopping in a grocery store in Rio, a white customer pushed past us to get in the front of the line. Maséqua told him, "We are standing here. Get back in line behind me." It was clear we were not from Brazil; his shock was apparent. He was obviously accustomed to disrespecting people of color in Brazil and getting away with it, but we were not the ones. A similar thing happened when we were at a concession stand at a park.

A Branco (White) guy walked up and got in front of me in line. After letting him know I wasn't having it, he backed up. It was time to return to the U.S. for a familiar type of racism.

Pelourinho is the historic center of Salvador da Bahia. Pelourinho means whipping post where slaves were punished. - Photo credit: Maséqua

Our trip to Rio de Janeiro, Brazil, was not as impressive as the visit to Salvador da Bahia. Rio was more of a tourist trap of beaches and naked bodies and was not as historically focused.

We did visit Candelária Church where a mass killing of homeless children took place on July 23, 1993. During that night, eight homeless people, including six minors, were killed by a group of men beside the Candelária Church. Our hearts bled as our tour guide explained what happened before and following this incident.

When Blackness was Golden

On the morning of July 22, 1993, the day before the massacre, a group of homeless children threw stones at police cars. We were also told that local merchants hired a "hit squad" to eliminate the roaming homeless children problem. At midnight, several cars with covered license plates stopped in front of the church where a group of roughly seventy street children, mostly Black boys, were sleeping. Shooters emerged from the cars and opened fire, killing eight and wounding dozens. Several of the men were police officers and were put on trial for the killings, but only two were ever convicted.

This monument in Rio is dedicated to murdered homeless teens. The outlines are of the bodies where they had been sleeping when shot. Photo credit: Maséqua

Chapter Sixteen: Back in Chicago

Following my father's death and our work in Trinidad and Tobago, Maséqua and I stayed in Chicago. Maséqua's mother was getting older, and we thought it would be good to remain close for her. My mother's health was already deteriorating when she developed small cell lung cancer and passed. I wrote this poem in my parents' memory:

> The Last Time
> (For my mom and dad)
>
> The last time I saw him was winter
> No snow in Chicago just wind and cold.
> I held his hand firmly and said not to worry
> As he took his last breath and passed on.
> The last time I saw her was springtime
> On a bright sunny day in Philadelphia,
> Surrounded by flowers lying on a white ruffled pillow
> wearing a bone-colored dress
> Soft music playing in the background
> The last time I saw them was today
> smiling in the recesses of my mind.
> Mom and Dad holding hands
> I miss them!
>
> Pemon Rami - April 4, 2009

One thing I enjoyed about returning home to Chicago was there was no telling who I'd run into. One such encounter happened at the airport when I ran into Dr. Wayne Watson, who was then-chancellor of the City Colleges of Chicago. Wayne reminded me I had cast him in a movie *(Mahogany)* when he was a student.

Another encounter took place at Dominic's Grocery store in South Shore when we ran into Dr. Carol Adams. At that time, Carol was secretary of the Department of Human Services, the state's largest government agency. Dr. Adams is a "heart and soul" community leader, always organizing, building, and moving toward next-level progress. When we told her we had moved back to Chicago, she asked if Maséqua and I would be interested in developing a project for DHS. Of course, we said yes!

So, in the fall of 2003, Maséqua and I created *Productions to Change Lives* (P2CL) with assistance and support from the Illinois Department of Human Services. P2CL became the prototype for development of the Teen Talk Radio Theatre Apprenticeship Program. P2CL is a training and production model that focused on integrating art and media through the eyes of teens to effect community involvement and positive change.

The Teen Talk Radio Theatre Apprentice Program was first presented at Paul Robeson High School and supported by the After School Matters program for two and a half years (Spring 2004 through Spring 2006).

Teen Talk Radio Theatre was a weekly radio talk show broadcast on WHPK 88.5 FM Chicago and WKKC 89.3 FM. The program was designed for teens to write, engineer, and produce radio plays about hot topics concerning teens. It included hosting a call-in segment that gave teens a chance to voice their opinions and seek solutions.

Our mission concerning youth has always been to provide a forum for teens to apply their talents to communicate their ideas, investigate their thoughts, and look toward the future in ways to uplift their communities.

Maséqua and I taught teens the importance of giving back to their communities and society in general. We taught them how to broaden their perspectives. As we explained to them, when you look out of the window you must train your eyes to not only see broken glass and misery but also the beauty and flowers growing.

Several of the over 700 members of our apprenticeship and radio broadcast programs included: Zon D Amour, Natalie Battles, Chance the Rapper, Justin Cuttingham, Zon D'Amour, Ja'Mal Green, Lashaun Johnson, Lexi Leggs, DaVante Lovett, Corey Mason, Shani Pitchford, No Name, Ricky Robinson, Billy Stevenson, and the Davis brothers Lennell and Terrell.

PRODUCTION AND SCREENING PHOTOS

Stories From the Soul TV show

In December 2006, Robert Townsend requested we create and produce a TV series for the Black Family Channel when he was CEO and president. The network was started by Florida attorney and philanthropist Willie E. Gary, former all-star baseball player Cecil Fielder, heavyweight boxing champ Evander Holyfield, Marlon Jackson of the Jackson Family, and broadcast television veteran Alvin James. We created Stories from the Soul in honor of the oral tradition of storytelling of ancient African griots. Stories from the Soul was contemporary storytelling that reached deep within and often had life-changing effects. Each half-hour TV show highlighted guest celebrity performers and professional actors who interpreted stories from all walks of life, revealing different cultures, pain, love, traditions, disappointments, and expectations. Most of all, they offered soul-revealing stories that share people's commonalities.

The episodes were filmed at the Negro League Café on Forty-Third Street in Chicago. Our production partners included Don Curry and Michael Clay. We completed filming the first three episodes; however, the Black Family channel struggled with securing advertising support and operational funds and ceased operations before the episodes could air. On April 30, 2007, the Black Family Channel's programming and subscriber base was sold to the Gospel Music Channel.

Chapter Seventeen: Of Boys and Men

Around August 2006, Shebeta Carter called to ask if I would be interested in producing a feature film to be shot in Chicago. She explained that Robert Townsend had requested my assistance on-site to plan the production, hire staff, and set-up production offices. He also wanted a liaison between him and the first-time executive producers for the film.

After reading the script, I agreed. I knew the executive producer, Shebeta Carter. She had worked with me as an actress in the early seventies. Shebeta and her daughter Maisha had formed a non-profit organization, Anointed Harvesters. With the help of her brother, then-State Senator Rickey Hendon, they had received a grant of one million dollars to produce their first film. Robert had been invited to executive produce the low-budget feature and told the executive producers he would agree if they hired me to produce the project. The film, written by Chicagoan Michelle Amor, was originally titled *The Summer of '85*, a coming-of-age story about three young men and their summer of growing up. When we started working on the script, Robert decided to make the movie contemporary due to the limited budget because shooting a period film would be too costly.

Shebeta's daughter-in-law had been killed in an automobile accident, and Robert and I realized their real-life story had become a mirror of the imaginary movie we were trying to make. Along with Michelle, the writer, we talked for a couple of emotionally filled hours about their experience and impact of the death of their loved one. The film was then rewritten as Of Boys and Men; it also became more about the father.

I called Robert and suggested he consider playing the father in the film. When Maséqua and I produced *Spotlight on Actors* in L.A., Robert performed a dramatic piece, so I was sure he could handle the role. Maisha and Shebeta were not as sure and wanted Bernie Mac to play the father. I convinced them, however, and Robert agreed.

Of Boys and Men centered on the Coles family, a tightly knit African-American family with three children supported by their mother Rieta (Angela Bassett) and father Holden (Robert Townsend). When Rieta is killed in a car accident, Holden is left to raise the children. Through their struggles to cope with their loss, they learn important lessons about manhood and family.

Carl Seaton, originally from Chicago but living in L.A., was hired and was elated to direct the film. Carl had directed the highly acclaimed film, *One Week*.

The film was scheduled for an eighteen-day shoot in Chicago. With Robert on board playing the father, Angela Bassett, Victoria Rowell, Faizon Love, and Bobbie J. Thompson all agreed to join the cast. Joe "Jody" Williams was hired as director of photography. I really had to fight for Jody to get the job because a director of photography had been identified in L.A.!

On location shooting *Of Boys and Men* with Victoria Rowell, Robert Townsend and Angela Bassett. Photo credit: Tacuma Rami

The grant stated there would be an intern training program alongside the film, and Maséqua was hired to design and administer the program. Robert and Carl were often at odds. Keeping them from erupting was a challenge. The filming was completed on schedule and Katina Zinner was selected to edit the film in Los Angeles. The film was released by Warner Brothers Home Video.

The year 2010 ended like 1950 began, with me back in Provident Hospital where I was born. Sixty years later, I was back and being treated by Dr. Winston Burke for a leg wound that had developed because of my car accident. The healing required a wound vac, and I needed to be hospitalized for that care. I was released from the hospital right before the Kwanzaa holidays. I looked forward to 2011 with expectation and joy so our saga could continue.

Chapter Eighteen: The DuSable Museum

One guest we invited to be interviewed by the teens on our Teen Talk Radio Theatre radio show was the esteemed educator Dr. Carol Adams, who by then had become the CEO and president of the DuSable Museum of African-American History. Following the interview, Dr. Adams mentioned to me that the museum had an open position for a director of Education and Public Programs, and she suggested I apply.

On May 2, 2011, I began my journey as director of Education and Public Programs. Although I had never worked at a museum, I had managed many non-profit institutions. My job responsibilities were numerous, including supervising the education department's staff and serving as the chief spokesperson for the museum's educational and public programs. I also provided vision, strategic direction, and leadership to ensure the development and execution of the museum's lifelong learning educational portfolio.

With Dr. Carol Adams enjoying one of our many programs at the DuSable

The education programs included Chicago public schools, distance learning, digital media development, docent training, museum tour interpretation, e-learning, and outreach programs.

When I joined the staff, the museum was experiencing financial issues. Like many non-profit organizations, the museum was suffering with an unmotivated board of directors and costly overhead. The education and programs department I headed was funded for specific programs, but those were hampered by the need for general operating funds.

As CEO and president, Dr. Adams was following a troubled administration and was faced with multiple issues needing to be addressed. Dr. Adams and I were on the same page ideologically, and we were both fully committed to the museum and the Black community. There was never an issue about what we should do; it was only about whether we had the resources.

My five years at the DuSable Museum were full of great programming, including some of my favorites:

Girls Take Flight — Day-long event featuring Dr. Mae Jemison, designed to empower young girls through the remarkable stories of courage of African-American women in aviation and aerospace history.

Table of Brotherhood Panel — A panel discussion I served on for Chevrolet's Table of Brotherhood Project in preparation for the Dr. Martin Luther King Jr. memorial weekend in Washington, DC, moderated by Roland Martin.

The Ugandan Orphans Choir — The choir comprised five girls and five boys who were orphans from Uganda. Their show featured singing, drumming, and brought awareness and hope to poverty-stricken children around the world.

Dark Girls Documentary and Lecture — Dark Girls from directors Bill Duke and D. Channsin Berry, plus a panel discussion explored the deep-seated biases and attitudes about skin color.

Interview of Ta-Nehisi Coates — I had the pleasure of interviewing Ta-Nehisi Coates regarding his essay, "The Case for Reparations," published in The Atlantic.

Interview of Actor Delroy Lindo — On-stage interview of actor Delroy Lindo as part of the Question Bridge exhibition. Question Bridge is a documentary-style video art installation that aimed to represent and redefine Black male identity in America.

Formed a partnership with Ava DuVernay and AFFRM.COM as their Chicago film distribution partner

Kwanzaa Forgotten History Lecture Series — This program featured the founder of Kwanzaa, Dr. Maulana Karenga, Professor and Chair, Department of Africana Studies, California State University—Long Beach

Created the "Walking with Heroes" program, which featured actors reenacting historic and notable figures as part of a living exhibit. Actors portrayed baseball great Jackie Robinson, civil rights activist Rosa Parks, aviatrix Bessie Coleman, a porter from the Pullman Sleeping Car Company, and Nichelle Nichols (Lieutenant Uhura from Star Trek).

Civil War Re-Enactments — In 2013 and 2014, we turned the north lawn of DuSable Museum of African American History into a Civil War-era battlefield complete with cannon fire and Buffalo Soldiers, Union "Yankees" Soldiers, and Confederate "Rebel" soldiers.

When Blackness was Golden

The Trillion-Dollar Question–Panel Discussion — an essential and timely discussion inspired by the findings exposed in "The State of the African American Consumer," a consumer report by Nielsen, which revealed that the buying power of African Americans was expected to reach $1 trillion by 2015.

Discovering DuSable Digitally — Discovering DuSable digitally was created to develop short films, a website, and curriculum designed for middle school students, teachers, and parents.

The projects, written by David Barr, focused on Jean Baptiste Pointe DuSable, the pioneer who established the first non-indigenous settlement in the area that would become Chicago. David's full-length play, The Face of Emmett Till (formerly The State of Mississippi vs Emmett Till), was developed with Mrs. Mamie Till Mobley and is based on the life and tragic death of her son, Emmett Till.

Maséqua and Associates was hired to produce the series of reenactments and documentary segments to be filmed in Chicago, Haiti, and Louisiana.

Edgar Miguel Sanchez as Jean Baptist Pointe DuSable and Jordan L. Gurneau as Choctaw

Chapter Nineteen: Louisiana and Haiti

To tell the story of Jean Baptiste Pointe DuSable, as supervising producer for the DuSable Museum of African American History I commissioned David Barr to write the script, Jim Quattrocki as the director of photography, Jonathan Woods to direct the reenactments, and Maséqua Myers as producer/director. The plan was to shoot in Chicago, Louisiana, and then Haiti, and that's what we did. For the Chicago shoot, Maséqua recruited Perry Thompson and Big River Productions to provide horses and riders for the project. Edger Sanchez was cast as DuSable, and we worked with the American Indian Center in Chicago to provide Native American actors and additional authentic resources, such as costumes and props, for the project.

The Bayou River Teche view from Breaux Bridge

In Louisiana, we worked with Professor Jihad Muhammad, founder of the African Scientific Research Institute (ASRI). This organization conducts world-class research dedicated to identifying ancient burial sites and tracing the historical footsteps of early African ancestors, both free and enslaved, who lived in America during 1628-1888.

In 1999, Brother Muhammad and ASRI had begun the search for Jean Baptiste Pointe DuSable's burial site. Muhammad joined the DuSable's documentary team in search of enslaved African historical routes of entry and escape as well as African and African-American burial sites in Louisiana.

Maséqua interviewing Professor Jihad Muhammad in Lafayette, Louisiana

Filming took place in Lafayette, St. Martin Parish, Breaux Bridge, and St. Martinville. The Bayou River Teche is a 125-mile-long waterway that was the demarcations points for many slave ships arriving in Louisiana.

Seeing the swamp land was bone chilling in 2012 while imagining what a group of African people forcibly taken from their home must have felt. Being brought to this extremely strange place and having no idea what was going to happen to them had to be horrifying. These were the thoughts that went through some of the crew's mind.

When Blackness was Golden

As the crew was traveling slowly through the swamps by boat, at times the river looked foreboding with the enormous hanging branches from the moss trees, leaves and roots of other trees, and plants that camouflage snakes, alligators, or other predators. Other times, the bayous provided a sense of calm, warmth, and beauty. For the crew to reach the burial sites required a boat because many of the graves are hidden deep in the woods behind plantations that still belong to the same families that owned the slaves. While the crew was preparing to return to Chicago, the deadly and destructive tropical cyclone Hurricane Isaac came ashore with intense rains and winds of eighty miles per hour. Because of the storm, the crew ended up stranded in Louisiana for an additional week.

Haiti

The final phase of the travel plan for the documentary took us to Saint-Marc, north of Port-au-Prince, Haiti, where DuSable was born. I decided to join the crew there. We had arranged for an interpreter/guide to meet us at the airport and work with us for the length of our stay. When we arrived, he was nowhere to be found and did not answer his phone when we called. So, we had to navigate the best we could. We were overrun in the baggage claim area by Haitians grabbing for our luggage and arguing over who was going to pick us up and become our driver.

One of the first Haitians who approached us that spoke English wore tons of gold chains and came off like a shyster. We were then introduced to an older gentleman who spoke English but was legally blind. He explained he knew exactly where we were going, and he could get us to our hotel. We agreed to go with the older man when we discovered he had a driver! The expected time to drive to St. Marc from the airport was a little under two hours, mostly on dark back roads. It was scary to be in a foreign country and not speak the language, but we made it without being kidnapped or worse!

Photo taken at the airport in Haiti Photo credit: Jim Quattrocki

Haiti is incredibly beautiful; however, so much of the land is comparatively neglected and some neighborhoods are a challenge to live in because of poverty and crime. Yet, despite the man-made problems coupled with the natural disasters that has hit the land, the spirit and resilience of the people is mind-boggling. This resilient spirit is evident in the people and the children, teachers, and administrators we met when visiting the Lycée Jean-Baptiste Pointe-du-Sable School.

Hand in Hand for Haiti is a collective that responded to the humanitarian crisis in Haiti following the catastrophic earthquake that hit the country on January 12, 2010. The founders set out to build a sustainable school complex that offered a high-quality education for the neediest children of the city of Saint-Marc. The school is open to the community and education is so affordable that attending school is possible for even the poorest of families.

When Blackness was Golden

Recruitment of students is based on the principle of equal opportunity and open to children from all backgrounds, without social discrimination.

We toured the museum in Port-au-Prince, Musée du Panthéon National Haitien (MUPANAH), which is located across the street from the National Palace. As director of education at the DuSable Museum, I was amazed at the discipline and order the young students maintained while

Standing on DuSable Street in Port-au-Prince, Haiti
Photo credit: Jim Quattrocki

waiting outside in the sweltering heat to get into the building.

The young students were quiet, orderly, and attentive, unlike many of the school groups that toured the DuSable. The Discovering DuSable Digitally project was funded by Chase Bank.

When we visited the college, we found students sitting in classrooms studying intensely despite parts of the ceiling missing, no lighting, and floors damaged by the earthquake.

Haiti became the world's first Black-led independent Caribbean state when it overthrew the French colonial control and slavery in the early nineteenth century. Haiti officially declared its independence in 1804 and has been constantly exploited since. On April 17, 1825, the King of France issued a decree stating France would only recognize Haitian independence if they were paid reparations of $21 billion.

When Blackness was Golden

That amount was to compensate the French colonists for their lost revenues from slavery. And Haiti to this day is still paying which contributes to the country being poor.

Interdisciplinary African and African American Studies

As the director of Education and Public Programs at the DuSable Museum, I had the honor of coordinating the development and implementation of the Interdisciplinary African and African American Studies curriculum for the Illinois State Board of Education.

In addition, I worked with Chicago Public Schools to develop its Interdisciplinary African and African American Studies Curriculum Guide for use from kindergarten through twelfth grade.

I had once again gone full circle, or should I say the circle was again completed!

When I was organizing the citywide boycotts of CPS in 1968, I never imagined that forty-six years later, I would be supervising the development and implementation of the mandated CPS Interdisciplinary African and African American Studies curriculum in 2014.

In October 2014, it was announced that Dr. Adams would be leaving the DuSable Museum, and I knew it was a matter of time before I would leave, too. I had come to realize that non-profit organizations are very often leadership-driven.

It is the heart, commitment, and brilliance of directors that drive the work and achievements.

Most community-based leaders start with a cause or a determination to solve an issue for the love of the community served. However, when they depart, the heart and passion leaves with them. Many times, the person taking over operates mainly from their head. Money, as opposed to commitment, becomes the priority. Inefficiency sets in, services weaken, and staff commitment and institutional histories are often ignored.

The great Oscar Brown Jr., while visiting our home in L.A. years ago, asked me a question I have never forgotten: "Do you think it is by accident that all the wrong people run our institutions?"

After Dr. Adams' departure, one of the board members was assigned to become interim president. Accomplished businessman Robert Blackwell took over the day-to-day operations until the board could secure a new CEO. My relationship with Blackwell was professional and supportive. I continued to produce public programs and completed more curriculum units for the State Board of Education until then-Governor Bruce Rauner froze the remaining $75,000 funding that was promised to the DuSable Museum for the Amistad commission programming.

When Blackness was Golden

After cutting the Amistad funding, Rauner and his wife donated $1,000 to the museum. I considered it a slap in the face!

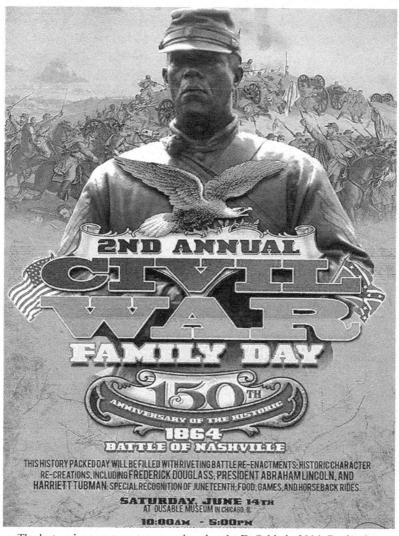

The last major event my team produced at the DuSable in 2014. Design by: Courtney Jolliff

Chapter Twenty: Lagos, Nigeria

I first became interested in visiting Nigeria and exploring its culture in 1966, when I was introduced to the *Drums of Passion* album by Babatundé Olatunji. At the time, I was a member of a Latin percussion group named the Exotics. When our members heard the album, it changed the direction of our group, and my life shifted toward a path of African exploration. Our eldest son (born in 1970) was given a Yoruba name, Babatunde Olugbala. Our second son (born in 1976) was named Tacuma Akintunde. Our granddaughter's, (Tacuma's daughter), name is Nigeria. Coincidence? I don't think so!

On May 5, 2015, Maséqua and I arrived at Murtala Muhammed International Airport in Lagos to begin the celebration of our fortieth wedding anniversary. The airport was crowded with international travelers going heretofore. The colorful clothing, the smell of African food, and the unique sounds of the city let us know we were in Africa, the cradle of civilization!

We navigated through the crowded airport to the customer service desk and were greeted by an intelligent, pleasant young lady who assisted us in getting through customs, exchanging money, and finding a driver to take us to our hotel. And with that, our adventure began! When we arrived in Lagos (after a stopover in Paris), it was following a torrential rainstorm. The streets were flooded, and traffic was at a standstill!

We had recently traveled to Haiti, and the traffic there was so bad I promised I would never complain again about traffic. But then we arrived in Lagos. The promise of not complaining about traffic only lasted until I got back home to Chicago and its freeways! Oh well!

When Blackness was Golden

As I mentioned, traffic was horrendous, but our young driver knew every route, backstreet, and alley to get us to our hotel. The trip from the airport to our hotel, which should have taken one hour, took five and a half because of the rain-flooded streets!

But we were home in Africa—specifically Lagos—and we were excited! The Four Points Sheraton was the five-star hotel we selected for the first part of our stay. The hotel was beautiful and the staff accommodating. The hotel was on Victoria Island in an affluent area that is also the main business and financial center of Lagos. There was live entertainment at the hotel along with poolside meals of incredible food which kept us at the hotel enjoying and taking it all in for the rest of the evening. The following morning, we were greeted with sunshine. Though the hotel was terrific, tempting us to stay inside, we decided to venture out and stroll to see what we could see in Lagos.

We walked across the street from the hotel and began negotiating with the drivers who had availability to provide all-day transportation and be our personal driver for a week. The young man we selected was not only courteous and friendly but also very knowledgeable about the Lagos, Nigerian history, and places we should visit.

As a filmmaker and historian, I couldn't help but be caught up in the sights of the city and the countryside. Some highlights of our trip included:

The Nigerian National Museum which was both eye-opening and engaging. The museum has an incredible collection of Nigerian art, including pieces of statuary, carvings, archaeological, and ethnographic exhibits. A terracotta human head known as the Jemaa Head (c. 900 to 200 BC), part of the Nok culture, is located at Onikan, Lagos Island.

The terra-cotta piece is named after the village where it was uncovered. The museum's "Circle of Life" exhibit is also worth mentioning and was very informative.

It covers the historic African ethology from birth, family, elderhood, and death.

We visited Freedom Park, a memorial and leisure park area in the middle of downtown Lagos, which was formerly Her Majesty's Broad Street Prison. The onstage entertainment and the tour of the former prison was enlightening.

Our driver suggested we also visit Niké's Art Centre, a four-story art gallery with breathtaking African art. We were greeted by gallery owner, artist, and designer Niké Davies Okundayé, who was both warm and welcoming. Her personal care and treatment of visitors is impressive as she welcomes and engulfs them in African attire and dance. Niké invited us to travel with her to Oshogbo to visit her home, studio, and school, where textile artists, painters, sculptors, and craftsmen carry out their trades and global visitors come to study. We also viewed her students making indigo tie-dyed fabrics with all-natural ingredients.

When Blackness was Golden

We visited Ikoyi, one of the most affluent communities in Lagos. Maséqua, me and Niké Davies Okundayé, owner of Niké Art Gallery

Another highlight was the Lekki Market with its unique artwork and crafts. I particularly liked the traditional masks we purchased. Prices were fantastic! One of our other objectives for the trip was to visit the city of Ifé, an ancient Yoruba city in southwestern Nigeria, we had studied as teens. The city is in the present-day Osun State and dates back to around 500 B. C. Ilé Ifé is the city where the Yoruba believe their civilization began. The Yoruba temple I frequented in Chicago in the late '60s was named Ilé Ifé.

Upon arrival in Ifé, we were greeted by drummers and dancers. We had the honor of meeting the Ooni of Ile-Ife, the traditional ruler of the Yoruba kingdom of Ile-Ife.

To experience a different part of Lagos, we changed hotels, moving to The Avenue Suites on Victoria Island. Following one of our many excursions, we returned to the hotel and discovered an information card in our room with a listing of things to do while in Lagos.

We came across a site to visit called Terra Kulture, which was walking distance from the hotel. It was our last full day in Lagos, so we visited, and our relationship with Lagos changed forever. Terra Kulture is an incredible facility and production company. We started our visit in their food court with a delicious meal. We then purchased art in the gallery, African cloth, books, and gifts in the library bookstore.

As we were leaving Terra Kulture, I asked the staff member sitting at the cash register if we could meet the owner. At the time of our visit, I was the director of Education and Public Programs at the DuSable, the oldest African-American museum in the United States.

Terra Kulture Arts and Studios is an educational and recreational organization which promotes the richness and diversity of Nigerian languages, arts and culture. Photo credit: Maséqua

But it was Maséqua's role as the executive director of the South Side Community Art Center, the oldest independently Black-owned art center in the USA, that really sealed the meeting. The receptionist told us the owner would see us but only for a few minutes.

When Blackness was Golden

Bolanle Austen-Peters was a joy to meet. Aside from being the founder of Terra Kulture, Bolanle is one of Nigeria's most prolific theatre and movie directors and producers. She has pioneered the national and international re-emergence of the Nigerian theatre industry. What was originally to be a meeting for a few minutes turned into a two-hour visit. We had much in common, and we clicked immediately. I had no idea a few months later that I would return to Nigeria to join Bolanle and the production team to produce the feature film 93 Days.

93 Days producing team Steve Gukas (Director), Bolanle Austen-Peters, and Dotun Olakunri - Photo credit: Barrett Akpokabayen

Culture is all about the people; in Nigeria, the people are everything. To fully describe my experience in Nigeria would require its own book so I will leave that for later.

When I returned to the museum from our vacation, I informed the DuSable's interim president Bob Blackwell of the opportunity that had arose in Nigeria and that I would be returning to produce the film. I asked if he would prefer, I resign or take a leave of absence.

Bob suggested I take the leave, which I did. So, it was back to Nigeria for three months!

The Feature Film - *93 Days*

In August 2015, I returned to Lagos to commence production of the film 93 Days. The movie centered on the true-life stories of men and women who risked their lives and sacrificed to save people from the consequences of the highly dreaded Ebola virus outbreak.

In 2007, Maséqua and I received the Chicago African American Arts Alliance Lifetime Achievement Award for our contributions to the development of films, television productions, music concerts, theatre, documentaries, and multimedia designs for institutions in Chicago and across the country. Following the award show, we met a young filmmaker named Adedapo Akisanya who won outstanding film producer for his film ESP that night. We were so impressed with Ade and his talents that Maséqua and I hired him for several projects over the years. As part of my continued mentoring and giving back, I hired Ade as the first assistant director for 93 Days and had him come to Nigeria for four months to assist me in making the film. Ade's parents are Nigerian and were born there while he was born in the United States. Having Ade on board in Nigeria was a blessing. His work ethic, calm demeanor, and organizational skills were invaluable.

On September 13, 2016, *93 Days* premiered at the Rock Cathedral in Lekki, Lagos, for an audience of 7,000 people.

IT'S A WRAP.

By the time I returned to Chicago from Nigeria, the DuSable Museum had hired a new president. From my first day back at the museum, she completely ignored me as she called meetings with the department staff I headed.

I was not invited. The vibes were strange, and the general staff meetings were dictatorial and tense.

In mid-October, the new president informed me the position I held as director of Education and Public Programs and my department had been eliminated. She then said, "You will need to clear out your office today." I was shocked at first, especially since we had never had a meeting. "I understand you have the right to decide who your staff will be, but I will not be treated like I've committed a crime. Based on my work history and contributions to this museum, I deserve more respect. If this is the way you're going to act, I will call a press conference in front of the museum and inform the community of your unwarranted actions." She decided to be civil. "How much time do you need to transition out?" I responded "the end of the year feels about right." So, I officially left at the end of the year.

93 Days was being edited in London, so I got on a plane and headed there. Our film was selected for premiering and viewing at many of the major film festivals, including:

- Toronto International Film Festival
- Chicago International Film Festival
- Pan African Film Festival in Los Angeles, at which I received the festival's Visionary Producer Award
- Johannesburg Film Festival
- Africa Film Festival in Cologne/Germany and nominated for a Rapid Lion Award

93 Days received the highest number of nominations in the 2017 Africa Magic Viewer's Choice Awards. The film received thirteen nominations and won the award for best lighting designer. Also nominated in seven categories for the 2017 African Movie Academy Awards, *93 Days* was the highest nominated film that year.

In the U.S., 93 Days aired on Netflix and Amazon Prime. My greatest joy came from seeing a gigantic poster for the film hanging on the side of a building in Nigeria with my name on it.

Black Harvest Film Festival

On August 4, 2018, Maséqua and I were thrilled to be the co-recipients of the Deloris Jordan Award for Excellence in Community Leadership presented on opening night at the twenty-fourth annual Black Harvest Film Festival held at the Gene Siskel Film Center in Chicago.

The Deloris Jordan award is presented by basketball hall of famer Michael Jordan's mother. A few of the past recipients include Roger and Chaz Ebert, Merri Dee, Warner Saunders, Common, Rhymefest a.k.a. Che Smith, and Regina Taylor.

When Blackness was Golden

Receiving the Deloris Jordan award at the Black Harvest Film Festival

What was one of the best of times in my life being in Africa turned into a different reality when I returned to Chicago. My doctor informed me they had diagnosed me with prostate cancer. When I received that information, my mind went blank. I felt a sense of impending doom as thoughts of my life ending rushed in.

I reached out to actor and producer Tim Reid, with whom I had just worked on 93 Days.

Tim is a prostate cancer survivor and was very helpful in providing resources to study and contacts to consult. I had a radical prostatectomy which is an operation to remove the prostate gland rather than go through chemotherapy. The procedure was a success, and the prostate cancer has not reappeared so far. Receiving the cancer diagnosis was like a kick in the gut. My first thought was what do I need to accomplish before I run out of time, as if my doctor had told me I had a limited amount of time to live. My next thought was this was just another challenge I needed to get around.

A year or two later, I was diagnosed with the beginning stages of liver cancer, for which I am currently being treated. The cancer is under control, and I show no physical symptoms, so my life's work will continue as I mentor and continue to share my knowledge with the up-and-coming next generation of artists.

When I started my journey to write this memoir, I received the advice that a person's story never ends until death, so I needed to determine when this part of my story should end. It is hard to imagine that when I was born during the 1950s Black men were constantly terrorized and could not present themselves as men. By the 1960s that began to change as Black men began to stand up straight and reclaim their manhood. The death of Trayvon Martin, Breonna Taylor and George Floyd, among so many others, motivated a new generation of activists determined to make the world they inherited a better place. I am encouraged by the new Black leaders emerging and shining a new light on the tribulations we face. We must reclaim this world as a place where humans share it and where they have an appreciation for the value of life. We must stop looking down on each other and work together toward uplifting everyone. There is enough land, enough resources, and enough water to share globally.

I hope this book motivates people to realize it only takes one person to start a movement and make the right choices. What path you decide to take will have a great deal to do with what legacy you leave for generation after generation after generation. I realize each chapter could be its own book and maybe I will be able to delve more deeply in future writings. In the meantime, I will keep on doing what I do!

Maséqua and I were inducted into the 2018 HistoryMakers Archive

Maséqua and I have both grown from history seekers to History Makers and…our journey continues!

Afterword by Bolanle Austen-Peters

Bolanle Austen-Peters is a Nigerian movie and theatre producer, director and lawyer. Bolanle is the founder and managing director of Terra Kulture, the foremost Nigerian Art and Culture Centre in Lagos.

It was May 2015. I had a very busy day with a long list of meetings. It was getting tedious, so I wasn't entertaining any unscheduled meetings. My secretary walked in to inform me about an elderly couple who wanted to meet me. I initially declined, but he persisted that they were from Chicago (I have a thing for Chicago) so I reluctantly agreed on the proviso that it was for a few minutes.

The meeting of a few minutes became a few hours, and this changed the course of my creative direction. That meeting led to our working together on a movie, 93 Days, which achieved global recognition and awards. I am thankful for their unwavering support and knowledge during the period we shot the movie.

Mr. Rami is an embodiment of rich, historic Black knowledge, very suave and cultured. Ms. Maséqua Myers-Rami is one of the most resourceful artistic personalities I've met, and her knowledge about the arts is also incredible. At that time, she was the executive director of the South Side Community Art Center in Chicago. Together, they make a formidable pair.

It is an honor and pleasure for me to be recognized in Mr. Rami's memoir. He has an uncompromising love for work and an outstanding work ethic. His memory is incredible, and he is detailed, professional, and highly resourceful.

When Blackness was Golden

A great connector and networker, he introduced us to Ade, one of the best 1st ADs we ever met, and Mr. Tim Reid.

He smoothed the path with our working with Mr. Danny Glover.

Going through his memoir reveals his rich cultural journey and exposure. It reveals the reason history needs to be told and the reason his name will be celebrated for generations yet unborn. It is clear there is a future for Black theatre with more globally recognized African movies.

Pemon has done well in preserving history in his own way and has recorded the same in fine print. This is phenomenal. He has such a rare background that dates back to the time of Martin Luther King and even had the privilege of watching him deliver a speech.

We at Terra Kulture will continue preserving history by telling our stories through theatre productions, stage plays, and movies. We appreciate the synergy that was created and look forward to future work. Nigeria and Lagos will always be home to Mr. Rami. This book is a great read, worthy of every university library. It is rich in historical facts with clear pictorials dating back to the time when Blackness was golden.

A Few Thoughts About Pemon Rami
Barbara J. Ray Marshall, Ph.D.

Pemon Rami, o.k.a. (once known as) Anthony Dewey Ray, is my middle brother. Even as a young child, he always moved across spaces and between lines. Pemon cut across the grain and questioned authority. I remember that he fell on a piece of glass on the playground while playing basketball. I, being the big sister, rode with him to the hospital and remained in the examination room while he was getting stitches. He looked over at me while I was being lifted off the floor, shook his head, and asked, "Do you really want to be a nurse?" I opted to become a teacher. Pemon became a researcher in our family genealogy long before the search for roots became a popular topic. He has worn many hats: writer, actor, director, producer, mentor, husband, father, brother, and friend.

It is my honor to write this afterword for his memoir. He remembers things—incidents, events, and people—that I don't. Pemon has had a knack for interacting with the lives of Black folks in Chicago and in other places around the world where he has landed, either via plane or on foot. Pemon Rami has etched his own place in space, history, and time, and, in doing so, embraced the larger venue of life.

Awards, Boards and Commissions

Awards

African American Arts Alliance	Lifetime Achievement Award
Beverly Hills/Hollywood NAACP	Best Theatre Director Award
The Videographer Award	Award of Excellence
International Television Assoc.	First Place
Windows of Opportunity	Touch the Spirit Award
Arizona Health Association	First Place
International Television Assoc.	Award of Merit
American Advertising Federation	Gold Nugget Award
Mayor Coleman Young	Key to the City Detroit, Michigan
Detroit City Council	Proclamation
Los Angeles City Council	Proclamation
Pan African Film Festival	Visionary Feature Film Award
Chicago Defender Newspaper	Men of Excellence Award
Cedars-Sinai Medical Center	President's Award
Deloris Jordan/Black Harvest	Excellence in Comm. Leadership
Chicago Defender Newspaper	50 Men of Excellence Award
Cedars-Sinai Medical Center	President's Award
Albert Nelson Marquis	Lifetime Achievement Award
Wendell Phillips High School	Hall of Fame
African Film Academy	African Academy Award Nominee
African People's Choice Awards	Choice Award Nominee

Boards and Commissions

- Board Member – Illinois Arts Council
- Luminary Board - Independent Film Alliance
- Member, Illinois Great Migration Commission
- Member, Joseph Jefferson Awards Committee
- Member, Panasonic Advisory Committee
- Judge, Top 100 Producers – AV Video Multimedia Producer magazine
- Evaluator/Consultant, National Endowment of the Arts
- Consultant, Illinois Office of Motion Pictures
- Grant Panel Member, Arizona Commission on the Arts
- Grant Panel Member, Illinois Arts Council
- Grant Panel Member, Phoenix Arts Commission
- Board Member, Phoenix Festivals
- Founding Board Member, Midwest Black Theatre Alliance
- Founding Board Member, Chicago Black Theatre Alliance
- Founding Board Member, Chicago Theatre Alliance

Chronology of Creative Management

2020 thru present	Board Member – Illinois Arts Council
2019 (Six-months)	Temporary Theatre and Performance Programming Manager University of Chicago Green Line Performing Arts Center
2016 thru 2018	Member of the Joseph Jefferson Theatre Awards Committee
2011 thru 2016	Director of Education and Public Programs DuSable Museum of African American History
1992 thru 2000	Manager of Medical Media Cedars-Sinai Medical Center Los Angeles, California
1990 thru 1992	General Manager Marla Gibbs Vision Entertainment Complex Los Angeles.
1987 thru 1992	Manager of Audio-Visual Services Leadership Development Center – Phoenix, Arizona
1982 thru 1983	Managing/Artistic Director, Black Theatre Troupe - Phoenix, Az.
1973 thru 1979	Artistic/Managing Director, LaMont Zeno Theatre - Chicago, Ill.
1971 thru 1972	Artistic Director, Kuumba Workshop - Chicago, Ill.
1968 thru 1970	Associate Director South Side Center for the Performing Arts Chicago, Ill.

Index

93 Days, 162, 245, 246, 247, 248, 249

A

Abraham Lincoln Center, 45, 68, 112
Adedapo Akisaya, 246
Affro-Arts theater, 75
Allen Collard, 3, 18
Angela Bassett, 4, 199, 225
Arnell (Najwa) Pugh, 17, 145
Association for the Study of Negro Life and History, 42

B

Baba Alabi Ayinla, 58
Babatunde, 3, 103, 104, 171, 181, 187, 188, 241
Babatunde Graves, 17
Babatundé Olatunji, 57, 241
Berry Gordy, 8, 166, 167, 188
Big Time Buck White, 101, 102
Billy Dee Williams, 8, 31, 166, 167
Bird of an Iron Feather, 91
Black Arts Movement, 57, 69, 108
Black Belt, 21, 27, 32, 40, 51
Black Manifesto, 74, 75
Black Panther's, 40, 79
Black People's Topographical Research Center, 44
Black Power conference, 72, 74
Black Stone Rangers, 77
Black Theatre, 3, 60, 106
Black Theatre Troupe, 160, 176, 181, 186, 257
Blaxploitation films, 175
Blues Brothers, 155, 162, 168, 169, 174
Bob Crawford, 17
Bolanle Austin-Peters, 4, 245

Bronzeville, 27, 40, 42

C

Candelária Church, 217
Cedars-Sinai Medical Center, 188, 198, 199, 203, 255, 257
Chaka Khan, 4, 64
Chicago Defender, 3, 25, 91, 106, 157, 255
Cicely Tyson, 4, 168, 200
Clarence Taylor, 18, 113, 149, 150
Communiversity, 45
Cooley High, 8, 114, 162, 167
Crispus Attucks, 34, 39, 53, 55
Curtis Ellis, 19, 59

D

Danny Glover, 4, 190, 200
Daphne Maxell Reid, 164
David Barr, 230, 232
David McKnight, 97
Deloris Jordan Award, 248
Delroy Lindo, 229
Denzel Washington, 190, 199
Dewey Foster, 25
Diana Ross, 8, 166, 167
Dick Anthony Williams, 4, 26
Discovering DuSable Digitally, 230
Douglas Alan Mann, 17, 113, 148
Dr. Alvenia Fulton, 43
Dr. Anderson Thompson, 3, 18, 78, 146, 213, 216
Dr. Barbara Ann Teer, 103
Dr. Barbara Marshall, 53, 55
Dr. Barbara Sizemore, 3, 18, 78, 98
Dr. Bobby Wright, 3, 19, 78
Dr. Carol Adams, 220, 227
Dr. Dorothy Height, 4, 184

Dr. Harold Pates, 3, 78, 195
Dr. Martin Luther King, 32, 63, 75, 105, 228
DuSable High School, 35

E

eta Creative Arts Foundation, 147, 149
Exotics, 54, 59, 241
Experimental Black Actors Guild, 6, 113, 149

F

Fanny McConnell Ellison, 106
Francis Ward, 149
Fred Hampton, 18, 40, 78, 79

G

Gangster Disciples, 77
George Cleveland Hall Branch Library, 42
George Shirley, 25
Gloria Foster, 4, 185
Golden Shears Barbershop, 59
Great Migration, 25, 256
Grinnell College, 9

H

H. Rap Brown, 79, 80, 90
Haiti, 230, 232, 234, 235, 237, 241
Hammurabi Robb, 38, 41
Harold "Okoro" Johnson, 3
Harold Lee Rush, 4, 71, 114
Harold Ray, 17, 21, 81, 146
Harold Vick, 185
Helen Mason, 176
Hollywood Squares, 213
House of Knowledge, 38

I

Ile Ife, 42, 58, 66
Illinois Film Office, 170
Isaac Hayes, 166
Ivan Dixon, 4, 162, 164

J

Jacqueline Stewart, 165
James Earl Jones, 4, 31, 185, 192
Jean Baptiste Pointe DuSable, 35, 232, 233
Jeff Fort, 77
Jesse Jackson, 72, 185, 191
Jim Harvey, 3, 70, 73, 75, 80
Jim Quattrocki, 232
Jimmy Spinks, 17, 36
Joe Jody Williams, 225
John B. Calhoun, 33

K

Kalamazoo Civic Theatre, 155, 176
Kelan Phil Cohran, 3
Kuumba, 107, 108, 109, 110, 149, 150, 154, 257

L

L. Scott Caldwell, 143
Lagos, 241, 242, 243, 244, 246
LaMont Zeno Theatre, 8, 113, 115, 149, 152, 159, 257
Langston Hughes, 9, 40, 60, 62, 96, 106, 110
Lawrence Fishburne, 200
Leander Jones, 3, 17, 98
Lyrics of Sunshine and Shadow, 55, 56, 158

M

Madame Lily, 193
Mahogany, 8, 114, 166, 167, 188, 219
Malcolm X College, 112, 158

Marie Thérèse ditte Coincoin, 23
Mark Clark, 40, 79
Marla Gibbs, 4, 26, 52, 189, 257
Masequa, 3, 7, 9, 66, 67, 70, 72, 78, 79, 98, 99, 104, 107, 114, 143, 145, 146, 148, 149, 152, 153, 154, 155, 156, 159, 164, 176, 177, 178, 179, 180, 181, 182, 183, 184, 186, 188, 189, 190, 192, 193, 194, 196, 198, 202, 205, 206, 209, 210, 212, 216, 219, 220, 225, 226, 230, 251
Maulana Ron Karenga, 68
Michael Jones, 53
Michelle Amor, 224
Morgan Freeman, 4, 167
Muhammad Ali, 92, 101

N

National Black Theater, 103
National Film Registry, 165
Negro League Café, 223
Negro Leagues, 47
Niké's Art Centre, 243

O

Of Boys and Men, 162, 224
Okoro Harold Johnson, 3
One in a Million, 170, 171
Organization of Black American Culture, 43
Oscar Brown Jr, 3, 4, 18, 41, 55, 60, 62, 92, 101, 106, 149, 158, 159, 160, 170, 239
Oscar Ray Sr., 21
Owen Lawson, 71

P

Pekin Theatre, 105
Phil Cohran, 18, 44, 55
Professor Jihad Muhammad, 232
Provident Hospital, 21, 40, 226

R

Rahsaan Roland Kirk, 147
Rat Experiment, 33
Reuben Cannon, 190, 193, 200

Rev. Jesse Jackson, 77, 79
Rhonada "Masequa" Myers, 3
Rhonada Angelia Myers, 61
Richard Durham, 91, 92, 106
Robert Townsend, 4, 6, 113, 114, 143, 181, 190, 191, 193, 209, 212, 222, 224, 225
Roland Martin, 228
Ron Milner, 60, 98, 158, 193, 194
Royal Shakespearian Festival, 152

S

Salvador Bahia, 213
Sam Greenlee, 3, 4, 19, 41, 162, 170
Sammy Davis Jr., 4, 79, 105, 201
Sanford and Son, 189
Savannah Paramore, 21
Shebeta Carter, 224
Sister T.M. Myers, 66
Stateway Garden's, 37
Stateway Gardens Housing Projects, 29
Stores from the Soul, 222

T

Tacuma, 3, 181
Tacuma Akintunde, 150
Ta-Nehisi Coates, 229
Teen Talk Radio Theatre, 220, 221, 227
The Great Migration, 25
The Low End, 27
The Regal Theater, 105
The South Side Center for the Performing Arts, 43
The South Side Community Art Center, 42
The Spook Who Sat By The Door, 4, 115, 162
Theodore Ward, 3, 18, 41, 43, 95, 96, 100, 101, 106
Tim Reid, 164, 249
Trinidad and Tobago, 209, 210, 212, 219

U

Umoja Black Student Center, 66, 70, 73, 77, 78, 201

V

Val Gray Ward, 3, 107, 108, 110, 149, 150, 154
Vivian G. Harsh, 42

W

Wabash Avenue YMCA, 41
Wall of Respect, 15, 43
Wall of Truth, 15, 43, 44
Walter Valentine, 53
Wendell Phillips, 51, 52, 70, 74, 255
Where is the Pride What is the Joy, 7, 190
Whitman Mayo, 4, 103, 189, 192
William Walker, 43
Willie C. Myers, 3, 66
Wole Soyinka, 109, 114, 146, 155

Y

Yoruba Temple, 42, 58